T0276479

Speech Recognition and Processing: Algorithms and Applied Principles

Speech Recognition and Processing: Algorithms and Applied Principles

Edited by **Marcus Hintz**

LANRYE
INTERNATIONAL

New Jersey

Published by Clanrye International,
55 Van Reypen Street,
Jersey City, NJ 07306, USA
www.clanryeinternational.com

Speech Recognition and Processing: Algorithms and Applied Principles
Edited by Marcus Hintz

International Standard Book Number: 978-1-63240-471-8 (Hardback)

Contents

Preface

Every book is a source of knowledge and this one is no exception. The idea that led to the conceptualization of this book was the fact that the world is advancing rapidly; which makes it crucial to document the progress in every field. I am aware that a lot of data is already available, yet, there is a lot more to learn. Hence, I accepted the responsibility of editing this book and contributing my knowledge to the community.

Speech recognition technique has proven to be significantly beneficial in the domain of Artificial Intelligence. This book is based on speech processing and recognition. It consists of information provided by top researchers from Italy, Tunisia, India, Netherlands, Canada and Finland. Topics like speech recognition, noise cancellation, speech enhancement and emotion recognition have been described in this book. Important techniques like voice conversion and multi resolution spectral analysis have also been elucidated. The book consists of both original research works as well as surveys along with the applications of the technology in various scientific fields. The aim of this book is to serve as a good source of knowledge for students and researchers related to this field.

While editing this book, I had multiple visions for it. Then I finally narrowed down to make every chapter a sole standing text explaining a particular topic, so that they can be used independently. However, the umbrella subject sinews them into a common theme. This makes the book a unique platform of knowledge.

I would like to give the major credit of this book to the experts from every corner of the world, who took the time to share their expertise with us. Also, I owe the completion of this book to the never-ending support of my family, who supported me throughout the project.

Editor

A Real-Time Speech Enhancement Front-End for Multi-Talker Reverberated Scenarios

Rudy Rotili, Emanuele Principi, Stefano Squartini and Francesco Piazza

Università Politecnica delle Marche

Italy

1. Introduction

In the direct human interaction, the verbal and nonverbal communication modes play a fundamental role by jointly cooperating in assigning semantic and pragmatic contents to the conveyed message and by manipulating and interpreting the participants' cognitive and emotional states from the interactional contextual instance. In order to understand, model, analyse, and automatize such behaviours, converging competences from social and cognitive psychology, linguistic, philosophy, and computer science are needed.

The exchange of information (more or less conscious) that take place during interactions build up a new knowledge that often needs to be recalled, in order to be re-used, but sometime it also needs to be appropriately supported as it occurs. Currently, the international scientific research is strongly committed towards the realization of intelligent instruments able to recognize, process and store relevant interactional signals: The goal is not only to allow efficient use of the data retrospectively but also to assist and dynamically optimize the experience of interaction itself while it is being held. To this end, both verbal and nonverbal (gestures, facial expressions, gaze, etc.) communication modes can be exploited. Nevertheless, voice is still a popular choice due to informative content it carries: Words, emotions, dominance can all be detected by means of different kinds of speech processing techniques. Examples of projects exploiting this idea are CHIL (Waibel et al. (2004)), AMI-AMIDA (Renals (2005)) and CALO (Tur et al. (2010)).

The applicative scenario taken here as reference is a professional meeting, where the system can readily assists the participants and where the participants themselves do not have particular expectations on the forms of supports provided by the system. In this scenario, it is assumed that people are sitting around a table, and the system supports and enrich the conversation experience by projecting graphical information and keywords on a screen.

A complete architecture of such a system has been proposed and validated in (Principi et al. (2009); Rocchi et al. (2009)). It consists of three logical layers: Perception, Interpretation and Presentation. The Perception layer aims to achieve situational awareness in the workplace and is composed of two essential elements: Presence Detector and Speech Processing Unit. The first determines the operating states of the system: Presence (the system checks if there are people around the table); conversation (the system senses that a conversation is ongoing). The Speech Processing Unit processes the captured audio signals and identifies the keywords that are exploited by the system in order to decide which stimuli to project. It consists of two main components: The multi-channel front-end (speech enhancement) and the automatic speech recognizer (ASR).

The Interpretation module is responsible of the recognition of the ongoing conversation. At this level, semantic representation techniques are adopted in order to structure both the content of the conversation and how the discussion is linked to the speakers present around the table. Closely related to this module is the Presentation one that, based on conversational analysis just made, dynamically decides which stimuli have to be proposed and sent. The stimuli are classified in terms of conversation topics and on the basis of their recognition, they are selected and projected on the table.

The focus of this chapter is on the speech enhancement stage of the Speech Processing Unit and in particular on the set of algorithms constituting the front-end of the ASR. In a typical meeting scenario, participants' voices can be acquired through different type of microphones. Depending on the choice made, the microphone signals are more or less susceptible to the presence of noise, the interference from other co-existing sources and reverberation produced by multiple acoustic paths. The usage of close-talking microphones can mitigate the aforementioned problems but they are invasive and the meeting participants can feel uncomfortable in such situation. A less invasive and more flexible solution is the choice of far-field microphone arrays. In this situation, the extraction of a desired speech signal can be a difficult task since noise, interference and reverberation are more relevant.

In the literature, several solutions have been proposed in order to alleviate the problems (Naylor & Gaubitch (2010); Woelfel & McDonough (2009)): Here, the attention is on two popular techniques among them, namely blind source separation (BSS) and speech dereverberation. In (Huang et al. (2005)), a two stage approach leading to sequential source separation and speech dereverberation based on blind channel identification (BCI) is proposed. This can be accomplished by converting the multiple-input multiple-output (MIMO) system into several single-input multiple-output (SIMO) systems free of any interference from the other sources. Since each SIMO system is blindly identified at different time, the BSS algorithm does not suffer of the annoying permutation ambiguity problem. Finally, if the obtained SIMO systems room impulse responses (RIRs) do not share common zeros, dereverberation can be performed by using the Multiple-Input/Output Inverse Theorem (MINT) (Miyoshi & Kaneda (1988)).

A real-time implementation of this approach has been presented in (Rotili et al. (2010)), where the optimum inverse filtering approach is substituted by an iterative technique, which is computationally more efficient and allows the inversion of long RIRs in real-time applications (Rotili et al. (2008)). Iterative inversion is based on the well known steepest-descent algorithm, where a regularization parameter taking into account the presence of disturbances, makes the dereverberation more robust to RIRs fluctuations or estimation errors due to the BCI algorithm (Hikichi et al. (2007)).

The major drawback of such implementation is that the BCI stage need to know "who speaks when" in order to estimate the RIRs related to the right speaker. To overcome the problem, in this chapter a solution which exploits a speaker diarization system is proposed. Speaker diarization steers the BCI and the ASR, thus allowing the identification task to be accomplished directly on the microphone mixture.

The proposed framework, is developed on the NU-Tech platform (Squartini et al. (2005)), a freeware software which allows the efficient management of the audio stream by means of the ASIO interface. NU-Tech provides a useful plug-in architecture which has been exploited for the C++ implementation. Experiments performed over synthetic conditions at 16 kHz sampling rate confirm the real-time capabilities of the implemented architecture and its effectiveness as multi-channel front-end for the subsequent speech recognition engine. The chapter outline is the following. In Sec. 2 the speech enhancement front-end, aimed at separating and dereverberating the speech sources is described, whereas Sec. 3 details the ASR engine and its parametrization. Sec. 4 is targeted to discuss the simulations setup and performed experiments. Conclusions are drawn in Sec. 5.

2. Speech enhancement front-end

Let M be the number of independent speech sources and N the number of microphones. The relationship between them is described by an $M \times N$ MIMO FIR (finite impulse response) system. According to such a model, the n-th microphone signal at k-th sample time is:

$$x_n(k) = \sum_{m=1}^{M} \mathbf{h}_{nm}^T \mathbf{s}_m(k, L_h), \qquad k = 1, 2, ..., K, \quad n = 1, 2, ..., N \tag{1}$$

where $(\cdot)^T$ denotes the transpose operator and

$$\mathbf{s}_m(k, L_h) = [s_m(k) \ s_m(k-1) \ \cdots \ s_m(k - L_h + 1)]^T. \tag{2}$$

is the m-th source. The term

$$\mathbf{h}_{nm} = [h_{nm,0} \ h_{nm,1} \ \cdots \ h_{nm,L_h-1}]^T, \quad n = 1, 2, ..., N, \quad m = 1, 2, ..., M \tag{3}$$

is the L_h-taps RIR between the n-th microphone and the m-th source. Applying the z transform, Eq. 1 can be rewritten as:

$$X_n(z) = \sum_{m=1}^{M} H_{nm}(z) S_m(z), \qquad n = 1, 2, ..., N \tag{4}$$

where

$$H_{nm}(z) = \sum_{l=0}^{L_h-1} h_{nm,l} z^{-1}. \tag{5}$$

The objective is recovering the original clean speech sources s_m by means of a speech dereverberation approach: Indeed, it is necessary to automatically identify who is speaking, accordingly estimating the unknown RIRs and then apply a seperation and dereverberation process to restore the original speech quality.

The reference framework proposed in (Huang et al. (2005); Rotili et al. (2010)) consists of three main stages: source separation, speech dereverberation and BCI. Firstly source separation is accomplished by transforming the original MIMO system in a certain number of SIMO systems and secondly the separated sources (but still reverberated) pass through the dereverberation process yielding the final cleaned-up speech signals. In order to make the two procedures properly working, it is necessary to estimate the MIMO RIRs of the audio channels between the speech sources and the microphones by the usage of the BCI stage. As mentioned in the introductory section, this approach suffers from the BCI stage inability of estimating the RIRs without the knowledge of the speakers' activities. To overcome this disadvantage a speaker diarization system can be introduced to steer the BCI stage. The block diagram of the proposed framework is shown in Fig. 1 where $N = 3$ and $M = 2$ have been considered. Speaker Diarization takes as input the central microphone mixture and for each

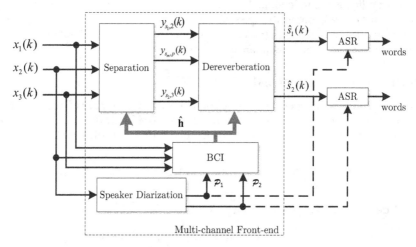

Fig. 1. Block diagram of the proposed framework.

frame, the output $\mathcal{P}_m$ is "1" if the m-th source is the only active, and "0" otherwise. In such a way, the front-end is able to detect when to perform or not to perform the required operation. Using the information carried out by the Speaker Diarization stage, the BCI will estimate the RIRs and the speech recognition engine will perform recognition if the corresponding source is the only active.

2.1 Blind channel identification

Considering a SIMO system for a specific source s_{m^*}, a BCI algorithm aims to find the RIRs vector $\mathbf{h}_{nm^*} = [\mathbf{h}_{1m^*}^T \ \mathbf{h}_{2m^*}^T \ \cdots \mathbf{h}_{Nm^*}^T]^T$ by using only the microphone signals $x_n(k)$. In order to ensure this, two identifiability condition are assumed satisfied (Xu et al. (1995)):

1. The polynomial formed from $\mathbf{h}_{nm^*}$ are co-prime, i.e. the room transfer functions (RTFs) $H_{nm^*}(z)$ do not share any common zeros (channel diversity);

2. $\mathcal{C}\{s(k)\} \geq 2L_h + 1$, where $\mathcal{C}\{s(k)\}$ denotes the linear complexity of the sequence $s(k)$.

This stage performs the BCI through the unconstrained normalized multi-channel frequency-domain least mean square (UNMCFLMS) algorithm (Huang & Benesty (2003)). It is an adaptive technique well suited to satisfy the real-time constraints imposed by the case study since it offers a good compromise among fast convergence, adaptivity, and low computational complexity.

Here, we briefly review the UNMCFLMS in order to understand the motivation of its choice in the proposed front-end. Refer to (Huang & Benesty (2003)) for details. The derivation of UNMCFLMS is based on cross relation criteria (Xu et al. (1995)) using the overlap-save technique (Oppenheim et al. (1999)).

The frequency-domain cost function for the q-th frame is defined as

$$J_f = \sum_{n=1}^{N-1} \sum_{i=i+1}^{N} \mathbf{e}_{ni}^H(q) \mathbf{e}_{ni}(q) \tag{6}$$

where $\mathbf{e}_{ni}(q)$ is the frequency-domain block error signal between the n-th and i-th channels and $(\cdot)^H$ denotes the Hermitian transpose operator. The update equation of the UNMCFLMS is expressed as

$$\widehat{\mathbf{h}}_{nm^*}(q+1) = \widehat{\mathbf{h}}_{nm^*}(q) - \rho[\mathbf{P}_{nm^*}(q) + \delta \mathbf{I}_{2L_h \times L_h}]^{-1}$$
$$\times \sum_{n=1}^{N} \mathbf{D}_{x_n}^H(q) \mathbf{e}_{ni}(q), \quad i = 1, \dots, N \tag{7}$$

where $0 < \rho < 2$ is the step-size, δ is a small positive number and

$$\widehat{\mathbf{h}}_{nm^*}(q) = \mathbf{F}_{2L_h \times 2L_h} \left[\widehat{\mathbf{h}}_{nm^*}(q) \ \mathbf{0}_{1 \times L_h} \right]^T,$$

$$\mathbf{e}_{ni}(q) = \mathbf{F}_{2L_h \times 2L_h} \left[\mathbf{0}_{1 \times L_h} \left\{ \mathbf{F}_{L_h \times L_h}^{-1} \mathbf{e}_{ni}(q) \right\}^T \right]^T,$$

$$\mathbf{P}_{nm^*}(q) = \sum_{n=1, n \neq i}^{N} \mathbf{D}_{x_n}^H(q) \mathbf{D}_{x_n}(q) \tag{8}$$

while $\mathbf{F}$ denotes the discrete Fourier transform (DFT) matrix. The frequency-domain error function $\mathbf{e}_{ni}(q)$ is given by

$$\mathbf{e}_{ni}(q) = \mathbf{D}_{x_n}(q)\widehat{\mathbf{h}}_{nm^*}(q) - \mathbf{D}_{x_i}(q)\widehat{\mathbf{h}}_{im^*}(q) \tag{9}$$

where the diagonal matrix

$$\mathbf{D}_{x_n}(q) = \mathrm{diag}\left(\mathbf{F}\left\{ [x_n(qL_h - L_h) \ x_n(qL_h - L_h + 1) \cdots x_n(qL_h + L_h - 1)]^T \right\} \right) \tag{10}$$

is the DFT of the q-th frame input signal block for the n-th channel. From a computational point of view, the UNMCFLMS algorithm ensures an efficient execution of the circular convolution by means of the fast Fourier transform (FFT). In addition, it can be easily implemented in a real-time application since the normalization matrix $\mathbf{P}_{nm^*}(q) + \delta \mathbf{I}_{2L_h \times L_h}$ is diagonal, and it is straightforward to compute its inverse.

Though UNMCFLMS allows the estimation of long RIRs, it requires a high input signal-to-noise ratio. In this paper, the presence of noise has not been taken into account and therefore the UNMCFLMS still remain an appropriate choice. Different solutions have been proposed in literature in order to alleviate the misconvergence problem of the UNMCFLMS in presence of noise. Among them, the algorithms presented in (Haque et al. (2007); Haque & Hasan (2008); Yu & Er (2004)) guarantee a significant robustness against noise and they could be used to improve our front-end.

2.2 Source separation

Here we briefly review the procedure already described in (Huang et al. (2005)) according to which it is possible to transform an $M \times N$ MIMO system (with $M < N$) in M $1 \times N$ SIMO systems free of interferences, as described by the following relation:

$$Y_{S_m,p}(z) = F_{S_m,p}(z)S_m(z) + B_{S_m,p}(z), \quad m = 1, 2, \ldots, M, \quad p = 1, 2, \ldots, P \qquad (11)$$

where $P = C_N^M$ is the number of combinations. It must be noted that the SIMO systems outputs are reverberated, likely more than the microphone signals due to the long impulse response of equivalent channels $F_{S_m,p}(z)$. Related formula and the detailed description of the algorithm can be found in (Huang et al. (2005)). Different choices can be made in order

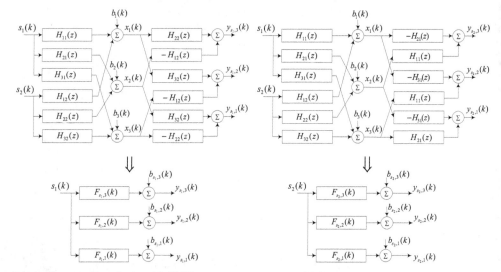

Fig. 2. Conversion of a 2×3 MIMO system in two 1×3 SIMO systems.

to calculate the equivalent SIMO system. In the block scheme of Fig. 2, representing the MIMO-SIMO conversion, is depicted a possible solution when $M = 2$ and $N = 3$. With this choice the first SIMO systems corresponding to the source s_1 is

$$F_{s_1,1}(z) = H_{32}(z)H_{21}(z) - H_{22}(z)H_{31}(z),$$
$$F_{s_1,2}(z) = H_{32}(z)H_{11}(z) - H_{12}(z)H_{31}(z),$$
$$F_{s_1,3}(z) = H_{22}(z)H_{11}(z) - H_{12}(z)H_{21}(z). \qquad (12)$$

The second SIMO system corresponding to the source s_2 can be found in a similar way, thus results, $F_{s_1,p}(z) = F_{s_2,p}(z)$ with $p = 1, 2, 3$. As stated in the previous section the presence of additive noise is not taken into account in this contribution and than all the terms $B_{S_m,p}(z)$ of Eq. 11 are equal to zero. Finally it is important to highlight that in using this separation algorithm a lower computation complexity w.r.t. traditional independent component analysis technique is achieved and since the MIMO system is decomposed into a number of SIMO systems which are be blindly identified at different time the permutation ambiguity problem is avoided.

2.3 Speech dereverberation

Given the equivalent SIMO system $F_{s_{m^*},p}(z)$ related to the specific source s_{m^*}, a set of inverse filters $G_{s_{m^*},p}(z)$ can be found by using the MINT theorem such that

$$\sum_{p=1}^{P} F_{s_{m^*},p}(z)G_{s_{m^*},p}(z) = 1, \tag{13}$$

assuming that the polynomials $F_{s_{m^*},p}(z)$ have no common zeros. In the time-domain, the inverse filter vector denoted as $\mathbf{g}_{s_{m^*}}$, is calculated by minimizing the following cost function:

$$C = \|\mathbf{F}_{s_{m^*}} \mathbf{g}_{s_{m^*}} - \mathbf{v}\|^2, \tag{14}$$

where $\| \cdot \|$ denote the l_2-norm operator and

$$\mathbf{g}_{s_{m^*}} = \left[\mathbf{g}_{s_{m^*},1}^T \ \mathbf{g}_{s_{m^*},2}^T \ \cdots \ \mathbf{g}_{s_{m^*},P}^T \right]^T, \tag{15}$$

$$\mathbf{g}_{s_{m^*},p} = \left[g_{s_{m^*},p}(1) \ g_{s_{m^*},p}(2) \ \cdots \ g_{s_{m^*},P}(L_g) \right]^T, \tag{16}$$

$$\mathbf{v} = [\underbrace{0, \cdots, 0}_{d}, 1, \cdots, 0]^T, \tag{17}$$

with $p = 1, 2, \cdots, P$. The vector $\mathbf{v}$ is the target vector, i.e. the Kronecker delta shifted by an appropriate modeling delay $(0 \leq d \leq PL_g)$ while $\mathbf{F}_{s_{m^*}} = \left[\mathbf{F}_{s_{m^*},1} \ \mathbf{F}_{s_{m^*},2} \ \cdots \ \mathbf{F}_{s_{m^*},P} \right]$ where $\mathbf{F}_{s_{m^*},p}$ is the convolution matrix of the equivalent FIR filter $\mathbf{f}_{s_{m^*},p} = \left[f_{s_{m^*},p}(1) \ f_{s_{m^*},p}(1) \ \cdots \ f_{s_{m^*},p}(L_f) \right]$ of length L_f. When the matrix $\mathbf{F}_{s_{m^*}}$ is obtained as shown in the previous section, the inverse filter set can be calculated as

$$\mathbf{g}_{s_{m^*}} = \mathbf{F}_{s_{m^*}}^\dagger \mathbf{v} \tag{18}$$

where $(\cdot)^\dagger$ denotes the Moore-Penrose pseudoinverse. In order to have a unique solution L_g must be chosen in such a way that $\mathbf{F}_{s_{m^*}}$ is square i.e.

$$L_g = \frac{L_f - 1}{P - 1}. \tag{19}$$

Considering the presence of disturbances, i.e. additive noise or RTFs fluctuations, the cost function Eq. 14 is modified as follows (Hikichi et al. (2007)):

$$C = \|\mathbf{F}_{s_{m^*}} \mathbf{g}_{s_{m^*}} - \mathbf{v}\|^2 + \gamma \|\mathbf{g}_{s_{m^*}}\|^2, \tag{20}$$

where the parameter $\gamma(\geq 0)$, called regularization parameter, is a scalar coefficient representing the weight assigned to the disturbance term. It should be noticed that Eq. 20 has the same form to that of Tikhonov regularization for ill-posed problems (Egger & Engl (2005)).

Let the RTF for the fluctuation case be given by the sum of two terms, the mean RTF ($\overline{\mathbf{F}}_{s_{m^*}}$) and the fluctuation from the mean RTF ($\widetilde{\mathbf{F}}_{s_{m^*}}$) and let $E\langle \widetilde{\mathbf{F}}_{s_{m^*}}^T \widetilde{\mathbf{F}}_{s_{m^*}} \rangle = \gamma \mathbf{I}$. In this case a general cost function, embedding noise and fluctuation case, can be derived:

$$C = \mathbf{g}_{s_{m*}}^T \mathcal{F}^T \mathcal{F} \mathbf{g}_{s_{m*}} - \mathbf{g}_{s_{m*}}^T \mathcal{F}^T \mathbf{v} - \mathbf{v}^T \mathcal{F} \mathbf{g}_{s_{m*}} + \mathbf{v}^T \mathbf{v} + \gamma \mathbf{g}_{s_{m*}}^T \mathbf{g}_{s_{m*}} \tag{21}$$

where

$$\mathcal{F} = \begin{cases} \mathbf{F}_{s_{m*}} & \text{(noise case)} \\ \overline{\mathbf{F}}_{s_{m*}} & \text{(fluctuation case).} \end{cases} \tag{22}$$

The filter that minimizes the cost function in Eq. 21 is obtained by taking derivatives with respect to $\mathbf{g}_{s_{m*}}$ and setting them equal to zero. The required solution is

$$\mathbf{g}_{s_{m*}} = \left(\mathcal{F}^T \mathcal{F} + \gamma \mathbf{I} \right)^{-1} \mathcal{F}^T \mathbf{v}. \tag{23}$$

The usage of Eq. 23 to calculate the inverse filters requires a matrix inversion that, in the case of long RIRs, can result in a high computational burden. Instead, an adaptive algorithm (Rotili et al. (2008)) has been here adopted to satisfy the real-time constraint. It is based on the steepest-descent technique, whose recursive estimator has the form

$$\mathbf{g}_{s_{m*}}(q+1) = \mathbf{g}_{s_{m*}}(q) - \frac{\mu(q)}{2} \nabla C. \tag{24}$$

Moving from Eq. 21 through simple algebraic calculations, the following expression is obtained:

$$\nabla C = -2[\mathcal{F}^T (\mathbf{v} - \mathcal{F} \mathbf{g}_{s_{m*}}(q)) - \gamma \mathbf{g}_{s_{m*}}(q)]. \tag{25}$$

Substituting Eq. 25 into Eq. 24 is

$$\mathbf{g}_{s_{m*}}(q+1) = \mathbf{g}_{s_{m*}}(q) + \mu(q)[\mathcal{F}^T (\mathbf{v} - \mathcal{F} \mathbf{g}_{s_{m*}}(q)) - \gamma \mathbf{g}_{s_{m*}}(q)], \tag{26}$$

where $\mu(q)$ is the step-size. The convergence of the algorithm to the optimal solution is guaranteed if the usual conditions for the step-size in terms of autocorrelation matrix $\mathcal{F}^T \mathcal{F}$ eigenvalues hold. However, the achievement of the optimum can be slow if a fixed step-size value is chosen. The algorithm convergence speed can be increased following the approach in (Guillaume et al. (2005)), where the step-size is chosen in order to minimize the cost function at the next iteration. The analytical expression obtained for the step-size is the following:

$$\mu(q) = \frac{\mathbf{e}^T(q) \mathbf{e}(q)}{\mathbf{e}^T(q) \left(\mathcal{F}^T \mathcal{F} + \gamma I \right) \mathbf{e}(q)} \tag{27}$$

where

$$\mathbf{e}(q) = \mathcal{F}^T \left[\mathbf{v} - \mathcal{F} \mathbf{g}_{s_{m*}}(q) \right] - \gamma \mathbf{g}_{s_{m*}}(q).$$

In using the previously illustrated algorithm, different advantages are obtained: The regularization parameter which takes into account the presence of disturbances, makes the dereverberation process more robust to estimation errors due to the BCI algorithm (Hikichi et al. (2007)); the real-time constraint can be met also in the case of long RIRs since no matrix inversion is required. Finally, the complexity of the algorithm has been decreased computing the required operation in the frequency-domain by using FFTs.

2.4 Speaker diarization

The speaker diarization stage drives the BCI and the ASRs so that they can operate into speaker-homogeneous regions. Current state-of-the-art speaker diarization systems are based on clustering approaches, usually combining hidden Markov models (HMMs) and the bayesian information criterion metric (Fredouille et al. (2009); Wooters & Huijbregts (2008)). Despite their state-of-art performance, such systems have the drawback of operating on the entire signals, making them unsuitable to work online as required by the proposed framework.

The approach taken here as reference has been proposed in (Vinyals & Friedland (2008)), and its block scheme for $M = 2$ and $N = 3$, is shown in Fig. 3. The algorithm operation is divided in two phases, training and recognition. In the first, the acquired signals, after a manual removal of silence periods, are transformed in feature vectors composed of 19 mel-frequency cepstral coefficients (MFCC) plus their first and second derivatives. Cepstral mean normalization is applied to deal with stationary channel effects. Speaker models are represented by mixture of Gaussians trained by means of the expectation maximization algorithm. The number of Gaussians and the end accuracy at convergence have been empirically determined, and set to 100 and 10^{-4} respectively. In this phase the voice activity detector (VAD) is also trained. The adopted VAD is based on bi-gaussian model of the log-energy frame. During the training a two gaussian model is estimated using the input sequence: The gaussian with the smallest mean will model the silence frames whereas the other gaussian corresponds to frames of speech activity.

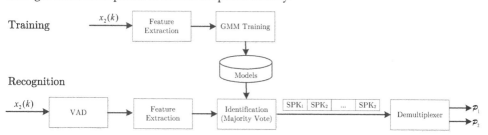

Fig. 3. The speaker diarization block scheme: "SPK$_1$" and "SPK$_2$" are the speaker identities labels assigned to each chunk.

In the recognition phase, the first operation consists in a voice activity detection in order to remove the silence periods: frames are tagged as silence or not based on the bi-gaussian model, using a maximum likelihood criterion.

After the voice activity detection, the signals are divided into non overlapping chunks, and the same feature extraction pipeline of the training phase extracts feature vectors. The decision is then taken using majority vote on the likelihoods: every feature vector in the current segment is assigned to one of the known speaker's model based on the maximum likelihood criterion. The model which has the majority of vectors assigned determines the speaker identity on the current segment. The Demultiplexer block associates each speaker label to a distinct output and sets it to "1" if the speaker is the only active, and "0" otherwise.

It is worth pointing out that the speaker diarization algorithm is not able to detect overlapped speech, and an oracle overlap detector is used to overcome this lack.

2.5 Speech enhancement front-end operation

The proposed front-end requires an initial training phase where each speaker is asked to talk for 60 s. During this period, the speaker diarization stage trains the both the VAD and speakers' models.

In the testing phase, the input signal is divided into non overlapping chunks of 2 s, the speaker diarization stage provides as output the speakers' activity $\mathcal{P}_m$. This information is employed both in the BCI stage and ASR engines: only when the m-th source is the only active the related RIRs are updated and the dereverberated speech recognized. In all the other situations the BCI stage provide as output the RIRs estimated at the previous step while the ASRs are idle.

The Separation stage takes as input the microphone signals and outputs the interference free signals that are subsequently processed by Dereverberation stage. Both stages perform theirs operations using the RIRs vector provided by the BCI stage.

The front-end performances are strictly related to the speaker diarization errors. In particular, the BCI stage is sensitive to false alarms (speaker in hypothesis but not in reference) and speaker errors (mapped reference is not the same as hypothesis speaker). If one of these occurs, the BCI performs the adaptation of the RIRs using an inappropriate input frame providing as output an incorrect estimation. An additional error which produces the previously highlighted behaviour is the miss speaker overlap detection.

The sensitivity to false alarms and speaker errors could be reduced imposing a constraint in the estimation procedure and updating the RIR only when a decrease in the cost function occurs. A solution to miss overlap error would be to add an overlap detector and not to perform the estimation if more than one speaker is simultaneously active. On the other hand, missed speaker errors (speaker in reference but not in hypothesis) does not negatively affect the RIRs estimation procedure, since the BCI stage does not perform the adaptation in such frames. Only a reduced convergence rate can be noticed in this case.

The real-time capabilities of the proposed front-end have been evaluated calculating the real-time factor on a Intel® Core™i7 machine running at 3 GHz with 4 GB of RAM. The obtained value for the speaker diarization stage is 0.03, meaning that a new result is output every 2.06 s. The real-time factor for the others stage is 0.04 resulting in a total value of 0.07 for the entire front-end.

3. ASR engine

Automatic speech recognition has been performed by means of the Hidden Markov Model Toolkit (HTK) (Young et al. (2006)) using HDecode, which has been specifically designed for large vocabulary speech recognition tasks. Features have been extracted through the HCopy tool, and are composed of 13 MFCC, deltas and double deltas, resulting in a 39 dimensional feature vector. Cepstral mean normalization is included in the feature extraction pipeline. Recognition has been performed based on the acoustic models available in (Vertanen (2006)).

The models differ with respect to the amount of training data, the use of word-internal or cross-word triphones, the number of tied states, the number of Gaussians per state, and the initialization strategy. The main focus of this work is to achieve real-time execution of the complete framework, thus an acoustic model able to obtain adequate accuracies and real-time ability was required. The computational cost strongly depends on the number of Gaussians per state, and in (Vertanen (2006)) it has been shown that real-time execution can be obtained using 16 Gaussians per state. The main parameters of the selected acoustic model are summarized in Table 1.

Training data	WSJ0 & WSJ1
Initialization strategy	TIMIT bootstrap
Triphone model	cross-word
# of tied states (approx.)	8000
# of Gaussians per state	16
# of silence Gaussians	32

Table 1. Characteristics of the selected acoustic model.

The language model consists of the 5k words bi-gram model included in the Wall Street Journal (WSJ) corpus. Recognizer parameters are the same as in (Vertanen (2006)): using such values, the word accuracy obtained on the November '92 test set is 94.30% with a real-time factor of 0.33 on the same hardware platform mentioned above. It is worth pointing out that the ASR engine and the front-end can jointly operate in real-time.

4. Experiments

4.1 Corpus description

The acoustic scenario under study is made of an array of three microphones and two speech sources located in a small office. The room arrangement is depicted in Fig. 4. The data set

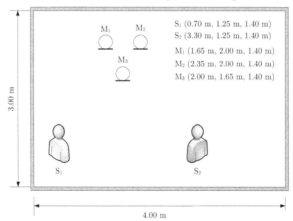

Fig. 4. Room setup.

used for the speech recognition experiments has been constructed from the WSJ November '92 speech recognition evaluation set. It consists of 330 sentences (about 40 minutes of speech), uttered by eight different speakers, both male and female. The data set is recorded at 16 kHz and does not contain any additive noise or reverberation.

A suitable database representing the described scenario has been artificially created using the following procedure: The 330 clean sentences are firstly reduced to 320 in order to have the same number of sentences for each speaker. These are then convolved with RIRs generated using the RIR Generator tool (Habets (2008)). No background noise has been added. Two different reverberation conditions have been taken into account: the low and the and high reverberant ones, corresponding to $T_{60} = 120$ ms and $T_{60} = 240$ ms respectively (with RIRs 1024 taps long).

For each channel, the final overlapped and reverberated sentences have been obtained by coupling the sentences of two speakers. Following the WSJ November '92 notation, speaker 440 has been paired with 441, 442 with 443, etc. This choice makes possible to cover all the combinations of male and female speakers, resulting in 40 sentences per couple of speakers. The mean value of overlap has been fixed to 15% of the speech frames for the overall dataset. For each sentence the amount of overlap is obtained as a random value drown from the uniform distribution on the interval [12, 18]. This assumption allows the artificial database to reflect the frequency of overlapped speech in real-life scenarios such as two-party telephone conversation or meeting (Shriberg et al. (2000)).

4.2 Front-end evaluation

As stated in Sec. 2 the proposed speech enhancement front-end consists in four different stages. Here we focus the attention on the evaluation of the Speaker Diarization and BCI stages which represent the most crucial parts of the entire system. An extensive evaluation of the Separation and Dereverberation stages can be found in (Huang et al. (2005)) and (Rotili et al. (2008)) respectively.

The performance of the speaker diarization algorithms are measured by the diarization error rate[1] (DER). DER is defined by the following expression:

$$\text{DER} = \frac{\sum_{s=1}^{S} \text{dur}(s)(\max(N_{\text{ref}}(s), N_{\text{hyp}}(s)) - N_{\text{correct}}(s))}{\sum_{s=1}^{S} \text{dur}(s)N_{\text{ref}}(s)} \qquad (28)$$

where dur is the duration of the segment, S is the total number of segments in which no speaker change occurs, $N_{\text{ref}}(s)$ and $N_{\text{hyp}}(s)$ indicate respectively the number of speakers in the reference and in the hypothesis, and $N_{\text{correct}}(s)$ indicates the number of speakers that speak in the segment s and have been correctly matched between the reference and the hypothesis. As recommended by the National Institute for Standards and Technology (NIST), evaluation has been performed by means of the "md-eval" tool with a collar of 0.25 s around each segment to take into account timing errors in the reference. The same metric and tool are used to evaluate the VAD performance[2].

Performance for the sole VAD are reported in table Table 2. Table 3 shows the results obtained testing the speaker diarization algorithm on the clean signals, as well as on the two reverberated scenarios in the previous illustrated configurations. For the seek of comparison two different configurations have been considered:

* REAL SD w/ ORACAL-VAD: The speaker diarization system uses an "Oracle" VAD;

---

[1] http://www.itl.nist.gov/iad/mig/tests/rt/2004-fall/
[2] Details can be found in "*Spring 2005 (RT-05S) Rich Transcription Meeting Recognition Evaluation Plan*". The "md-eval" tool is available at http://www.itl.nist.gov/iad/mig//tools/

- REAL SD w/ REAL-VAD: The system described in Sec. 2.4.

The performance across the three scenarios are similar due to the matching of the training and testing conditions, and are consistent with (Vinyals & Friedland (2008)).

	Clean	$T_{60} = 120\,\text{ms}$	$T_{60} = 240\,\text{ms}$
REAL-VAD	1.85	1.96	1.68

Table 2. VAD error rate (%).

	Clean	$T_{60} = 120\,\text{ms}$	$T_{60} = 240\,\text{ms}$
REAL-SD w/ ORACLE-VAD	13.57	13.30	13.24
REAL-SD w/ REAL-VAD	15.20	15.20	14.73

Table 3. Speaker diarization error rate (%).

The BCI stage performance are evaluated by means of a channel-based measure called Normalized Projection Misalignment (NPM) (Morgan et al. (1998)) defined as

$$\text{NPM}(q) = 20 \log_{10} \left(\frac{\|\epsilon(q)\|}{\|\mathbf{h}\|} \right), \tag{29}$$

where

$$\epsilon(q) = \mathbf{h} - \frac{\mathbf{h}^T \widehat{\mathbf{h}}(q)}{\widehat{\mathbf{h}}^T(q)\widehat{\mathbf{h}}(q)} \widehat{\mathbf{h}}(q) \tag{30}$$

is the projection misalignment vector, $\mathbf{h}$ is the real RIR vector whereas $\widehat{\mathbf{h}}(q)$ is the estimated one at the q-th iteration, i.e. the frame index.

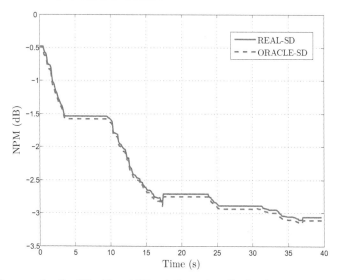

Fig. 5. NPM curves for the "Real" and "Oracle" speaker diarization system.

Fig. 5 shows the NPM curve for the identification of the RIRs relative to source s_1 at $T_{60} = 240\,\text{ms}$ for an input signal of 40 s. In order to understand how the performance of the Speaker Diarization stage affect the RIRs identification we compare the curves obtained for ORACLE-SD where the speaker diariazion operates in an "Oracle" fashion, i.e. it operates at 100% of its possibilities, and REAL-SD case. As expected the REAL-SD NPM is always above the ORACLE-SD NPM. Parts where the curves are flat indicate speech segment in which source s_1 is the not only active source i.e. it is overlapped to s_2 or we have silence.

4.3 Full system evaluation

In this section the objective is to evaluate the recognition capabilities of the ASR engine fed by speech signals coming from the multichannel DSP front-end, therefore the performance metric employed is the word recognition accuracy.

The word recognition accuracy obtained assuming ideal source separation and dereverberation is 93.60%. This situation will be denoted as "Reference" in the remainder of the section.

Four different setups have been addressed:

- Unprocessed: The recognition is performed on the reverberant speech mixture acquired from Mic_2 (see Fig. 4);
- ASR w/o SD: The ASRs do not exploit the speaker diarization output;
- ASR w/ ORACLE-SD: The ASRs exploit the "Oracle" speaker diarization output;
- ASR w/ REAL-SD: The ASRs exploit the "Real" speaker diarization output.

Fig. 6 reports the word accuracy for both the low and high reverberant conditions when the complete test file is processed by the multi-channel DSP front-end and recognition is performed on the separated and dereverberated streams (*Overall*) for all the three setup. Fig. 7 shows the word accuracy values attained where the recognition is performed starting from the first silence frame after the BCI and Dereverberation stages converge[3] (*Convergence*).

Observing the results of Fig. 6, it can be immediately stated that feeding the ASR engine with unprocessed audio files leads to very poor performances. The missing source separation and the related wrong matching between the speaker and the corresponding word transcriptions result in a significant amount of insertions which justify the occurrence of negative word accuracy values.

Conversely, when the audio streams are processed, the ASRs are able to recognize most of the spoken words, specially once the front-end algorithms have reached the convergence. The usage of speaker diarization information to drive the ASRs activity significantly increases the performance. As expected the usage of the "Real" speaker diarization instead of an "Oracle" one lead to a decrease in performance of about 15% for the low reverberant condition and of a 10% for the high reverberant condition. Despite this, the word accuracy is still higher then the one obtained without speaker diarization, providing an average increase of about 20% for both the reverberation time.

In the *Convergence* evaluation case study, when $T_{60} = 120\,\text{ms}$ and the "Oracle" speaker diarization is employed, a word accuracy of 86.49% is obtained, which is about 7% less than the result attainable in the "Reference" conditions. In this case, the usage of the "Real"

---

[3] Additional experiments have demonstrated that this is reached after $20 - 25$ s of speech activity.

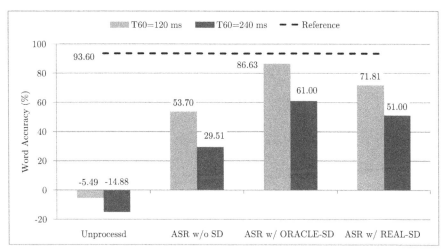

Fig. 6. Word accuracy for the *Overall* case.

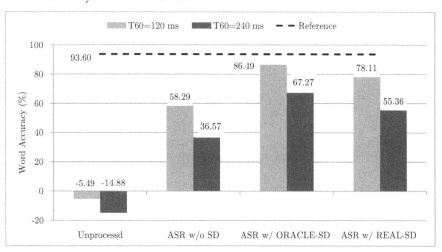

Fig. 7. Word accuracy for the *Convergence* case.

speaker diarization lead to decrease of only 8%. As expected, the reverberation effect has a negative impact on the recognition performances especially in presence of high reverberation, i.e. $T_{60} = 240$ ms. However, it must be observed that the convergence margin is even more significant w.r.t. the low reverberant scenario, further highlighting the effectiveness of the proposed algorithmic framework as multichannel front-end.

5. Conclusion

In this paper, an ASR system was successfully enhanced by an advanced multi-channel front-end to recognize the speech content coming from multiple speakers in reverberated acoustic conditions. The overall architecture is able to blindly identify the impulse responses, to separate the existing multiple overlapping sources, to dereverberate them and to recognize the information contained within the original utterances. A speaker diarization system able to steer the BCI stage and the ASRs has been also included in the overall framework. All the algorithms work in real-time and a PC-based implementation of them has been discussed in this contribution. Performed simulations, based on a existing large vocabulary database (WSJ) and suitably addressing the acoustic scenario under test, have shown the effectiveness of the developed system, making it appealing in real-life human-machine interaction scenarios. As future works, an overlap detector will be integrated in the speaker diarization system and its impact in terms of final recognition accuracy will be evaluated. In addition other applications different form ASR such as emotion recognition (Schuller et al. (2011)), dominance detection (Hung et al. (2011)) or keyword spotting (Wöllmer et al. (2011)) will be considered in order to assess the effectiveness of the front-end in other recognition tasks.

6. References

Egger, H. & Engl, H. (2005). Tikhonov regularization applied to the inverse problem of option pricing: convergence analysis and rates, *Inverse Problems* 21(3): 1027–1045.

Fredouille, C., Bozonnet, S. & Evans, N. (2009). The LIA-EURECOM RT'09 Speaker Diarization System, *RT'09, NIST Rich Transcription Workshop*, Melbourne, Florida, USA.

Guillaume, M., Grenier, Y. & Richard, G. (2005). Iterative algorithms for multichannel equalization in sound reproduction systems, *Proceedings of IEEE International Conference on Acoustics, Speech, and Signal Processing*, Vol. 3, pp. iii/269–iii/272.

Habets, E. (2008). Room impulse response (RIR) generator. URL: *http://home.tiscali.nl/ehabets/rirgenerator.html*

Haque, M., Bashar, M. S., Naylor, P., Hirose, K. & Hasan, M. K. (2007). Energy constrained frequency-domain normalized LMS algorithm for blind channel identification, *Signal, Image and Video Processing* 1(3): 203–213.

Haque, M. & Hasan, M. K. (2008). Noise robust multichannel frequency-domain LMS algorithms for blind channel identification, *IEEE Signal Processing Letters* 15: 305–308.

Hikichi, T., Delcroix, M. & Miyoshi, M. (2007). Inverse filtering for speech dereverberation less sensitive to noise and room transfer function fluctuations, *EURASIP Journal on Advances in Signal Processing* 2007(1).

Huang, Y. & Benesty, J. (2003). A class of frequency-domain adaptive approaches to blind multichannel identification, *IEEE Transactions on Speech and Audio Processing* 51(1): 11–24.

Huang, Y., Benesty, J. & Chen, J. (2005). A Blind Channel Identification-Based Two-Stage Approach to Separation and Dereverberation of Speech Signals in a Reverberant Environment, *IEEE Transactions on Speech and Audio Processing* 13(5): 882–895.

Hung, H., Huang, Y., Friedland, G. & Gatica-Perez, D. (2011). Estimating dominance in multi-party meetings using speaker diarization, *IEEE Transactions on Audio, Speech, and Language Processing* 19(4): 847–860.

Miyoshi, M. & Kaneda, Y. (1988). Inverse filtering of room acoustics, *IEEE Transactions on Signal Processing* 36(2): 145–152.

Morgan, D., Benesty, J. & Sondhi, M. (1998). On the evaluation of estimated impulse responses, *IEEE Signal Processing Letters* 5(7): 174–176.

Naylor, P. & Gaubitch, N. (2010). *Speech Dereverberation*, Signals and Communication Technology, Springer.

Oppenheim, A. V., Schafer, R. W. & Buck, J. R. (1999). *Discrete-Time Signal Processing*, 2 edn, Prentice Hall, Upper Saddle River, NJ.

Principi, E., Cifani, S., Rocchi, C., Squartini, S. & Piazza, F. (2009). Keyword spotting based system for conversation fostering in tabletop scenarios: Preliminary evaluation, *Proc. of 2nd Conference on Human System Interactions*, pp. 216–219.

Renals, S. (2005). AMI: Augmented Multiparty Interaction, *Proc. NIST Meeting Transcription Workshop*.

Rocchi, C., Principi, E., Cifani, S., Rotili, R., Squartini, S. & Piazza, F. (2009). A real-time speech-interfaced system for group conversation modeling, *19th Italian Workshop on Neural Networks*, pp. 70–80.

Rotili, R., Cifani, S., Principi, E., Squartini, S. & Piazza, F. (2008). A robust iterative inverse filtering approach for speech dereverberation in presence of disturbances, *Proceedings of IEEE Asia Pacific Conference on Circuits and Systems*, pp. 434–437.

Rotili, R., De Simone, C., Perelli, A., Cifani, A. & Squartini, S. (2010). Joint multichannel blind speech separation and dereverberation: A real-time algorithmic implementation, *Proceedings of 6th International Conference on Intelligent Computing*, pp. 85–93.

Schuller, B., Batliner, A., Steidl, S. & Seppi, D. (2011). Recognising realistic emotions and affect in speech: state of the art and lessons learnt from the first challenge, *Speech Communication* .

Shriberg, E., Stolcke, A. & Baron, D. (2000). Observations on Overlap : Findings and Implications for Automatic Processing of Multi-Party Conversation, *Word Journal Of The International Linguistic Association* pp. 1–4.

Squartini, S., Ciavattini, E., Lattanzi, A., Zallocco, D., Bettarelli, F. & Piazza, F. (2005). NU-Tech: implementing DSP algorithms in a plug-in based software platform for real time audio applications, *Proceedings of 118th Convention of the Audio Engineering Society*.

Tur, G., Stolcke, A., Voss, L., Peters, S., Hakkani-Tur, D., Dowding, J., Favre, B., Fernandez, R., Frampton, M., Frandsen, M., Frederickson, C., Graciarena, M., Kintzing, D., Leveque, K., Mason, S., Niekrasz, J., Purver, M., Riedhammer, K., Shriberg, E., Tien, J., Vergyri, D. & Yang, F. (2010). The CALO meeting assistant system, *IEEE Trans. on Audio, Speech, and Lang. Process.*, 18(6): 1601 –1611.

Vertanen, K. (2006). Baseline WSJ acoustic models for HTK and Sphinx: Training recipes and recognition experiments, *Technical report*, Cavendish Laboratory, University of Cambridge.
URL: *http://www.keithv.com/software/htk/us/*

Vinyals, O. & Friedland, G. (2008). Towards semantic analysis of conversations: A system for the live identification of speakers in meetings, *Proceedings of IEEE International Conference on Semantic Computing*, pp. 426 –431.

Waibel, A., Steusloff, H., Stiefelhagen, R. & the CHIL Project Consortium (2004). CHIL: Computers in the Human Interaction Loop, *International Workshop on Image Analysis for Multimedia Interactive Services*.

Woelfel, M. & McDonough, J. (2009). *Distant Speech Recognition*, 1st edn, Wiley, New York.

Wöllmer, M., Marchi, E., Squartini, S. & Schuller, B. (2011). Multi-stream lstm-hmm decoding and histogram equalization for noise robust keyword spotting, *Cognitive Neurodynamics* 5: 253–264.

Wooters, C. & Huijbregts, M. (2008).   The ICSI RT07s Speaker Diarization System, *in*
    R. Stiefelhagen, R. Bowers & J. Fiscus (eds), *Multimodal Technologies for Perception*
    of Humans, Lecture Notes in Computer Science, Springer-Verlag, Berlin, Heidelberg,
    pp. 509–519.
Xu, G., Liu, H., Tong, L. & Kailath, T. (1995). A Least-Squares Approach to Blind Channel
    Identification, *IEEE Transactions On Signal Processing* 43(12): 2982–2993.
Young, S., Everman, G., Kershaw, D., Moore, G. & Odell, J. (2006). *The HTK Book*, Cambridge
    University Engineering.
Yu, Z. & Er, M. (2004). A robust adaptive blind multichannel identification algorithm for
    acoustic applications, *Proceedings of IEEE International Conference on Acoustics, Speech,*
    and Signal Processing, Vol. 2, pp. ii/25–ii/28.

2

Real-Time Dual-Microphone
Speech Enhancement

Trabelsi Abdelaziz, Boyer François-Raymond and Savaria Yvon
École Polytechnique de Montréal
Canada

1. Introduction

In various applications such as mobile communications and digital hearing aids, the presence of interfering noise may cause serious deterioration in the perceived quality of speech signals. Thus, there exists considerable interest in developing speech enhancement algorithms that solve the problem of noise reduction in order to make the compensated speech more pleasant to a human listener. The noise reduction problem in single and multiple microphone environments was extensively studied (Benesty et al., 2005; Ephraim. & Malah, 1984). Single microphone speech enhancement approaches often fail to yield satisfactory performance, in particular when the interfering noise statistics are time-varying. In contrast, multiple microphone systems provide superior performance over the single microphone schemes at the expense of a substantial increase of implementation complexity and computational cost.

This chapter addresses the problem of enhancing a speech signal corrupted with additive noise when observations from two microphones are available. It is organized as follows. The next section presents different well-known and state of the art noise reduction methods for speech enhancement. Section 3 surveys the spatial cross-power spectral density (CPSD) based noise reduction approach in the case of a dual-microphone arrangement. Also included in this section, the well known problems associated with the use of the CPSD-based approach. Section 4 describes the single channel noise spectrum estimation algorithm used to cope with the CPSD-based approach shortcomings, and uses this algorithm in conjunction with a soft-decision scheme to come up with the proposed method. We call the proposed method the modified CPSD (MCPSD) based approach. Based on minimum statistics, the noise power spectrum estimator seeks to provide a good tradeoff between the amount of noise reduction and the speech distortion, while attenuating the high energy correlated noise components (i.e., coherent direct path noise), especially in the low frequency range. Section 5 provides objective measures, speech spectrograms and subjective listening test results from experiments comparing the performance of the MCPSD-based method with the cross-spectral subtraction (CSS) based approach, which is a dual-microphone method previously reported in the literature. Finally, Section 6 concludes the chapter.

2. State of the art

There have been several approaches proposed in the literature to deal with the noise reduction problem in speech processing, with varying degrees of success. These approaches can generally be divided into two main categories. The first category uses a single microphone system and exploits information about the speech and noise signal statistics for enhancement. The most often used single microphone noise reduction approaches are the spectral subtraction method and its variants (O'Shaughnessy, 2000).

The second category of signal processing methods applicable to that situation involves using a microphone array system. These methods take advantage of the spatial discrimination of an array to separate speech from noise. The spatial information was exploited in (Kaneda & Tohyama, 1984) to develop a dual-microphone beamforming algorithm, which considers spatially uncorrelated noise field. This method was extended to an arbitrary number of microphones and combined with an adaptive Wiener filtering in (Zelinski, 1988, 1990) to further improve the output of the beamformer. The authors in (McCowan & Bourlard, 2003) have replaced the spatially uncorrelated noise field assumption by a more accurate model based on an assumed knowledge of the noise field coherence function, and extended the CPSD-based approach to develop a more appropriate postfiltering scheme. However, both methods overestimate the noise power spectral density at the beamformer's output and, thus, they are suboptimal in the Wiener sense (Simmer & Wasiljeff, 1992). In (Lefkimmiatis & Maragos, 2007), the authors have obtained a more accurate estimation of the noise power spectral density at the output of the beamformer proposed in (Simmer & Wasiljeff, 1992) by taking into account the noise reduction performed by the minimum variance distortionless response (MVDR) beamformer.

The generalized sidelobe canceller (GSC) method, initially introduced in (Griffiths & Jim, 1982), was considered for the implementation of adaptive beamformers in various applications. It was found that this method performs well in enhancing the signal-to-noise ratio (SNR) at the beamformer's output without introducing further distortion to the desired signal components (Guerin et al., 2003). However, the achievable noise reduction performance is limited by the amount of incoherent noise. To cope with the spatially incoherent noise components, a GSC based method that incorporates an adaptive Wiener filter in the look direction was proposed in (Fischer & Simmer, 1996). The authors in (Bitzer et al., 1999) have investigated the theoretical noise reduction limits of the GSC. They have shown that this structure performs well in anechoic rooms, but it does not work well in diffuse noise fields. By using a broadband array beamformer partitioned into several harmonically nested linear subarrays, the authors in (Fischer & Kammeyer, 1997) have shown that the resulting noise reduction system performance is nearly independent of the correlation properties of the noise field (i.e., the system is suitable for diffuse as well as for coherent noise field). The GSC array structure was further investigated in (Marro et al., 1998). In (Cohen, 2004), the author proposed to incorporate into the GSC beamformer a multichannel postfilter which is appropriate to work in nonstationary noise environments. To discriminate desired speech transients from interfering transients, he used both the GSC beamformer primary output and the reference noise signals. To get a real-time implementation of the method, the author suggested in an earlier paper (Cohen, 2003a), feeding back to the beamformer the discrimination decisions made by the postfilter.

In the dual-microphone noise reduction context, the authors in (Le Bouquin-Jannès et al., 1997) have proposed to modify both the Wiener and the coherence-magnitude based filters by including a cross-power spectrum estimation to take some correlated noise components into account. In this method, the cross-power spectral density of the two input signals was averaged during speech pauses and subtracted from the estimated CPSD in the presence of speech. In (Guerin et al., 2003), the authors have suggested an adaptive smoothing parameter estimator to determine the noise CPSD that should be used in the coherence-magnitude based filter. By evaluating the required overestimation for the noise CPSD, the authors showed that the musical noise (resulting from large fluctuations of the smoothing parameter between speech and non-speech periods) could be carefully controlled, especially during speech activity. A simple soft-decision scheme based on minimum statistics to estimate accurately the noise CPSD was proposed in (Zhang & Jia, 2005).

Considering ease of implementation and lower computational cost when compared with approaches requiring microphone arrays with more than two microphones, dual-microphone solutions are yet a promising class of speech enhancement systems due to their simpler array processing, which is expected to lead to lower power consumption, while still maintaining sufficiently good performance, in particular for compact portable applications (i.e., digital hearing aids, and hands-free telephones). The CPSD-based approach (Zelinski, 1988, 1990), the adaptive noise canceller (ANC) approach (Maj et al., 2006), (Berghe & Wooters, 1998), and the CSS-based approach (Guerin et al., 2003; Le Bouquin-Jannès et al., 1997; Zhang & Jia, 2005) are well-known examples. The former lacks robustness in a number of practical noise fields (i.e., coherent noise). The standard ANC method provides high speech distortion in the presence of crosstalk interferences between the two microphones. Formerly reported in the literature, the CSS-based approach provides interesting performance in a variety of noise fields. However, it lacks efficiency in dealing with highly nonstationary noises such as the multitalker babble. This issue will be further discussed later in this chapter.

3. CPSD-based noise reduction approach

This section introduces the signal model and gives a brief review of the CPSD-based approach in the case of a dual-microphone arrangement. Let $s(t)$ be a speech signal of interest, and let the signal vector $n(t) = [n_1(t) \ n_2(t)]^T$ denote two-channel noise signals at the output of two spatially separated microphones. The sampled noisy signal $x_m(i)$ observed at the mth microphone can then be modeled as

$$x_m(i) = s(i) + n_m(i), \quad m = 1, \ 2 \tag{1}$$

where i is the sampling time index. The observed noisy signals are segmented into overlapping time frames by applying a window function and they are transformed into the frequency domain using the short-time Fourier transform (STFT). Thus, we have for a given time frame:

$$X(k,l) = S(k,l) + N(k,l) \tag{2a}$$

where k is the frequency bin index, and l is the time index, and where

$$X(k,l) = [X_1(k,l) \ X_2(k,l)]^T \tag{2b}$$

$$N(k,l) = [N_1(k,l) \ N_2(k,l)]^T \tag{2c}$$

The CPSD-based noise reduction approach is derived from Wiener's theory, which solves the problem of optimal signal estimation in the mean-square error sense. The Wiener filter weights the spectral components of the noisy signal according to the signal-to-noise power spectral density ratio at individual frequencies given by:

$$W(k,l) = \frac{\Phi_{SS}(k,l)}{\Phi_{X_m X_m}(k,l)} \tag{3}$$

where $\Phi_{SS}(k,l)$ and $\Phi_{X_m X_m}(k,l)$ are respectively the power spectral densities (PSDs) of the desired signal and the input signal to the mth microphone.

For the formulation of the CPSD-based noise reduction approach, the following assumptions are made:

1. The noise signals are spatially uncorrelated, $E\{N_1^*(k,l) \cdot N_2(k,l)\} = 0$;
2. The desired signal $S(k,l)$ and the noise signal $N_m(k,l)$ are statistically independent random processes, $E\{S^*(k,l) \cdot N_m(k,l)\} = 0$, $m = 1, 2$;
3. The noise PSDs are the same on the two microphones.

Under those assumptions, the unknown PSD $\Phi_{SS}(k,l)$ in (3) can be obtained from the estimated spatial CPSD $\Phi_{X_1 X_2}(k,l)$ between microphone noisy signals. To improve the estimation, the estimated PSDs are averaged over the microphone pair, leading to the following transfer function:

$$\hat{W}(k,l) = \frac{\Re\{\hat{\Phi}_{X_1 X_2}(k,l)\}}{(\hat{\Phi}_{X_1 X_1}(k,l) + \hat{\Phi}_{X_2 X_2}(k,l))/2} \tag{4}$$

where $\Re\{\ \}$ is the real operator, and " ^ " denotes the estimated value. It should be noted that only the real part of the estimated CPSD in the numerator of equation (4) is used, based on the fact that both the auto-power spectral density of the speech signal and the spatial cross-power spectral density of a diffuse noise field are real functions.

There are three well known drawbacks associated with the use of the CPSD-based approach. First, the noise signals on different microphones often hold correlated components, especially in the low frequency range, as is the case in a diffuse noise field (Simmer et al., 1994). Second, such approach usually gives rise to an audible residual noise that has a cosine shaped power spectrum that is not pleasant to a human listener (Le Bouquin-Jannès et al., 1997). Third, applying the derived transfer function to the output signal of a conventional beamformer yields an effective reduction of the remaining noise components but at the expense of an increased noise bias, especially when the number of microphones is too large (Simmer & Wasiljeff, 1992). In the next section, we will focus our attention on estimating and discarding the residual and coherent noise components resulting from the use of the CPSD-based approach in the case of a dual-microphone arrangement. For such system, the overestimation of the noise power spectral density should not be a problem.

4. Dual-microphone speech enhancement system

In this section, we review the basic concepts of the noise power spectrum estimator algorithm on which the MCPSD method presented later, is based. Then, we use a variation of this algorithm in conjunction with a soft-decision scheme to cope with the CPSD-based approach shortcomings.

4.1 Noise power spectrum estimation

For highly nonstationary environments, such as the multitalker babble, the noise spectrum needs to be estimated and updated continuously to allow an effective noise reduction. A variety of methods were recently reported that continuously update the noise spectrum estimate while avoiding the need for explicit speech pause detection. In (Martin, 2001), a method known as the minimum statistics (MS) was proposed for estimating the noise spectrum by tracking the minimum of the noisy speech over a finite window. The author in (Cohen & Berdugo, 2002) suggested a minima controlled recursive algorithm (MCRA) which updates the noise spectrum estimate by tracking the noise-only periods of the noisy speech. These periods were found by comparing the ratio of the noisy speech to the local minimum against a fixed threshold. In the improved MCRA approach (Cohen, 2003b), a different approach was used to track the noise-only periods of the noisy signal based on the estimated speech-presence probability. Because of its ease of use that facilitates affordable (hardware, power and energy wise) real-time implementation, the MS method was considered for estimating the noise power spectrum.

The MS algorithm tracks the minima of a short term power estimate of the noisy signal within a time window of about 1 s. Let $\hat{P}(k,l)$ denote the smoothed spectrum of the squared magnitude of the noisy signal $X(k,l)$, estimated at frequency k and frame l according to the following first-order recursive averaging:

$$\hat{P}(k,l) = \hat{\alpha}(k,l) \cdot \hat{P}(k,l-1) + (1 - \hat{\alpha}(k,l)) \cdot |X(k,l)|^2 \qquad (5)$$

where $\hat{\alpha}(k,l)$ $(0 < \hat{\alpha}(k,l) < 1)$ is a time and frequency dependent smoothing parameter. The spectral minimum at each time and frequency index is obtained by tracking the minimum of D successive estimates of $\hat{P}(k,l)$, regardless of whether speech is present or not, and is given by the following equation:

$$\hat{P}_{\min}(k,l) = \min(\hat{P}_{\min}(k,l-1), \hat{P}(k,l)) \qquad (6)$$

Because the minimum value of a set of random variables is smaller than their average, the noise spectrum estimate is usually biased. Let $B_{\min}(k,l)$ denote the factor by which the minimum is smaller than the mean. This bias compensation factor is determined as a function of the minimum search window length D and the inverse normalized variance $Q_{eq}(k,l)$ of the smoothed spectrum estimate $\hat{P}(k,l)$. The resulting unbiased estimator of the noise spectrum $\hat{\sigma}_n^2(k,l)$ is then given by:

$$\hat{\sigma}_n^2(k,l) = B_{\min}(k,l) \cdot \hat{P}_{\min}(k,l) \tag{7}$$

To make the adaptation of the minimum estimate faster, the search window of D samples is subdivided into U subwindows of V samples ($D = U \cdot V$) and the noise PSD estimate is updated every V subsequent PSD estimates $\hat{P}(k,l)$. In case of a sudden increase in the noise floor, the noise PSD estimate is updated when a local minimum with amplitude in the vicinity of the overall minimum is detected. The minimum estimate, however, lags behind by at most $D + V$ samples when the noise power increases abruptly. It should be noted that the noise power estimator in (Martin, 2001) tends to underestimate the noise power, in particular when frame-wise processing with considerable frame overlap is performed. This underestimation problem is known and further investigation on the adjustment of the bias of the spectral minimum can be found in (Martin, 2006) and (Mauler & Martin, 2006).

4.2 Dual-microphone noise reduction system

Although the CPSD-based method has shown its effectiveness in various practical noise fields, its performance could be increased if the residual and coherent noise components were estimated and discarded from the output spectrum. In the MCPSD-based method, this is done by adding a noise power estimator in conjunction with a soft-decision scheme to achieve a good tradeoff between noise reduction and speech distortion, while still guaranteeing its real-time behavior. Fig. 1 shows an overview of the MCPSD-based system, which is described in details in this section.

We consider the case in which the average of the STFT magnitude spectra of the noisy observations received by the two microphones, $|Y(k,l)| = (|X_1(k,l)| + |X_2(k,l)|)/2$, is multiplied by a spectral gain function $G(k,l)$ for approximating the magnitude spectrum of the sound signal of interest, that is

$$|\hat{S}(k,l)| = G(k,l) \cdot |Y(k,l)| \tag{8}$$

The gain function $G(k,l)$ is obtained by using equation (4), and can be expressed in the following extended form as

$$G(k,l) = \frac{(|X_1(k,l)| \cdot |X_2(k,l)|) \cdot \cos(\Delta\phi(k,l))}{(|X_1(k,l)|^2 + |X_2(k,l)|^2)/2} \tag{9a}$$

where

$$\Delta\varphi(k,l) = \varphi_{X_1}(k,l) - \varphi_{X_2}(k,l) \tag{9b}$$

and where $\varphi_{X_1}(k,l)$ and $\varphi_{X_2}(k,l)$ denote the phase spectra of the STFTs of $X_1(k,l)$ and $X_2(k,l)$ respectively that satisfy the relationship $|\varphi_{X_1}(k,l) - \varphi_{X_2}(k,l)| < \pi/2$. In the implementation of the MCPSD-based approach, any negative values of the gain function $G(k,l)$ are reset to a minimum spectral floor, on the assumption that such frequencies cannot be recovered. Moreover, good results can be obtained when the gain function $G(k,l)$ is squared, which improves the signals selectivity (i.e., those coming from the direct path).

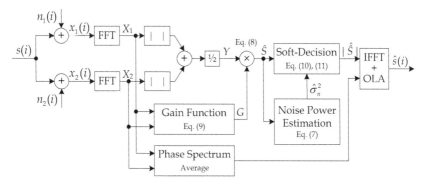

Fig. 1. The proposed dual-microphone noise reduction system for speech enhancement, where " | | " denotes the magnitude spectrum.

To track the residual and coherent noise components that are often present in the estimated spectrum in (8), a variation of the MS algorithm was implemented as follows. In performing the running spectral minima search, the D subsequent noise PSD estimates were divided into two sliding data subwindows of $D/2$ samples. Whenever $D/2$ samples were processed, the minimum of the current subwindow was stored for later use. The sub-band noise power estimate $\hat{\sigma}_n^2(k,l)$ was obtained by picking the minimum value of the current signal PSD estimate and the latest $D/2$ PSD values. The sub-band noise power was updated at each time step. As a result, a fast update of the minimum estimate was achieved in response to a falling noise power. In case of a rising noise power, the update of the minimum estimate was delayed by D samples. For accurate power estimates, the bias correction factor introduced in (Martin, 2001) was scaled by a constant decided empirically. This constant was obtained by performing the MS algorithm on a white noise signal so that the estimated output power had to match exactly that of the driving noise in the mean sense.

To discard the estimated residual and coherent noise components, a soft-decision scheme was implemented. For each frequency bin k and frame index l, the signal to noise ratio was estimated. The signal power was estimated from equation (8) and the noise power was the latest estimated value from equation (7). This ratio, called difference in level (DL), was calculated as follows:

$$DL = 10 \cdot \log_{10}\left(\frac{|\hat{S}(k,l)|^2}{\hat{\sigma}_n^2(k,l)} \right) \qquad (10)$$

The estimated DL value was then compared to a fixed threshold Th_s decided empirically. Based on that comparison, a running decision was taken by preserving the sound frequency bins of interest and reducing the noise bins to a minimum spectral floor. That is,

$$|\hat{S}(k,l)| = \begin{cases} |\tilde{S}(k,l)| \cdot \lambda \, , & \text{if } DL < 0 \\ |\tilde{S}(k,l)| \cdot \left(\left(\frac{DL}{Th_s} \right)^2 \cdot (1-\lambda) + \lambda \right) \, , & \text{if } DL < Th_s \\ |\tilde{S}(k,l)| \, , & \text{otherwise.} \end{cases} \qquad (11a)$$

where

$$|\tilde{S}(k,l)| = \sqrt{|\hat{S}(k,l)|^2 - \hat{\sigma}_n^2(k,l)} \qquad (11b)$$

and where λ was chosen such that $20 \cdot \log_{10}(\lambda) \cong -40$ dB. The argument of the square-root function in equation (11b) was restricted to positive values in order to guarantee real-valued results. When the estimated DL value is lower than the statistical threshold, the quadratic function "$(DL/Th_s)^2 \cdot (1-\lambda) + \lambda$" allows the estimated spectrum to be smoothed during noise reduction. It should be noted that the so called DL has to take positive values during speech activity and negative values during speech pause periods.

Finally, the estimated magnitude spectrum in (11) was combined with the average of the phase spectra of the two received signals prior to estimate the time signal of interest. In addition to the 6 dB reduction in phase noise, the time waveform resulting from such combination provided a better match of the sound signal of interest coming from the direct path. After an inverse DFT of the enhanced spectrum, the resultant time waveform was half-overlapped and added to adjacent processed segments to produce an approximation of the sound signal of interest (see Fig. 1).

5. Performance evaluation and results

This section presents the performance evaluation of the MCPSD-based method, as well as the results of experiments comparing this method with the CSS-based approach. In all the experiments, the analysis frame length was set to 1024 data samples (23 ms at 44.1 kHz sampling rate) with 50% overlap. The analysis and synthesis windows thus had a perfect reconstruction property (i.e., Hann-window). The sliding window length of D subsequent PSD estimates was set to 100 samples. The threshold Th_s was fixed to 5 dB. The recordings were made using a Presonus Firepod recording interface and two Shure KSM137 cardioid microphones placed approximately 20 cm apart. The experimental environment of the MCPSD is depicted in Fig. 2. The room with dimensions of 5.5 x 3.5 x 3 m enclosed a speech source situated at a distance of 0.5 m directly in front (0 degrees azimuth) of the input microphones, and a masking source of noise located at a distance of 0.5 m from the speech source.

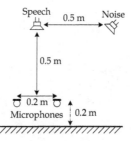

Fig. 2. Overhead view of the experimental environment.

Designed to be equally intelligible in noise, five sentences taken from the Hearing in Noise Test (HINT) database (Nilsson et al., 1994) were recorded at a sampling frequency of 44.1 kHz. They are

1. Sentence 1 (male talker): "Flowers grow in the garden".
2. Sentence 2 (female talker): "She looked in her mirror".
3. Sentence 3 (male talker): "The shop closes for lunch".
4. Sentence 4 (female talker): "The police helped the driver".
5. Sentence 5 (male talker): "A boy ran down the path".

Four different noise types, namely white Gaussian noise, helicopter rotor noise, impulsive noise and multitalker babble noise, were recorded at the same sampling rate and used throughout the experiments. The noise was scaled in power level and added acoustically to the above sentences with a varying SNR. A global SNR estimation of the input data was used. It was computed by averaging power over the whole length of the two observed signals with:

$$\text{SNR} = 10 \cdot \log_{10} \left(\frac{\sum\limits_{m=1}^{2}\sum\limits_{i=1}^{I} s^2(i)}{\sum\limits_{m=1}^{2}\sum\limits_{i=1}^{I} (x_m(i) - s(i))^2} \right) \tag{12}$$

where I is the number of data samples of the signal observed at the mth microphone. Throughout the experiments, the average of the two clean signals $s(i) = (s_1(i) + s_2(i))/2$ was used as the clean speech signal. Objective measures, speech spectrograms and subjective listening tests were used to demonstrate the performance improvement achieved with the MCPSD-based method over the CSS-based approach.

5.1 Objective measures

The Itakura-Saito (IS) distance (Itakura, 1975) and the log spectral distortion (LSD) (Mittal & Phamdo, 2000) were chosen to measure the differences between the clean and the test spectra. The IS distance has a correlation of 0.59 with subjective quality measures (Quakenbush et al., 1988). A typical range for the IS distance is 0–10, where lower values indicate better speech quality. The LSD provides reasonable degree of correlation with subjective results. A range of 0–15 dB was considered for the selected LSD, where the minimum value of LSD corresponds to the best speech quality. In addition to the IS and LSD measures, a frame-based segmental SNR was used which takes into consideration both speech distortion and noise reduction. In order to compute these measures, an utterance of the sentence 1 was processed through the two methods (i.e., the MCPSD and CSS). The input SNR was varied from −8 dB to 8 dB in 4 dB steps.

Values of the IS distance measure for various noise types and different input SNRs are presented in Tables 1 and 2 for signals processed by the different methods. Results in this table were obtained by averaging the IS distance values over the length of sentence 1. The results in this table indicate that the CSS-based approach yielded more speech distortion than that produced with the MCPSD-based method, particularly in helicopter and impulsive noise environments. Fig. 3 illustrates the comparative results in terms of LSD measures between both methods for various noise types and different input SNRs. From these figures, it can be observed that, whereas the two methods showed comparable improvement in the case of impulsive noise, the estimated LSD values provided by the MCPSD-based method were the lowest in all noise conditions. In terms of segmental SNR, the MCPSD-based method provided a performance improvement of about 2 dB on average, over the CSS-based approach. The largest improvement was achieved in the case of multitalker babble noise, while for impulsive noise this improvement was decreased. This is shown in Fig. 4.

SNR	White Noise			Helicopter Noise		
(dB)	CSS	MCPSD	Noisy	CSS	MCPSD	Noisy
−8	1.88	0.62	3.29	2.81	1.92	3.28
−4	1.4	0.43	2.82	2.18	1.29	2.62
0	0.78	0.3	2.23	1.72	0.95	2.18
4	0.51	0.24	1.64	1.28	0.71	1.7
8	0.34	0.25	1.18	0.87	0.47	1.24

Table 1. Comparative performance in terms of mean Itakura-Saito distance measure for white and helicopter noises and different input SNRs.

SNR	Impulsive Noise			Babble Noise		
(dB)	CSS	MCPSD	Noisy	CSS	MCPSD	Noisy
−8	2.71	2.03	3.23	2.38	1.26	3.1
−4	2.21	1.67	2.65	1.7	0.85	2.62
0	1.7	1.21	2.06	1.28	0.59	2.12
4	1.34	0.93	1.56	0.92	0.46	1.73
8	0.99	0.69	1.09	0.67	0.32	1.27

Table 2. Comparative performance in terms of mean Itakura-Saito distance measure for impulsive and babble noises and different input SNRs.

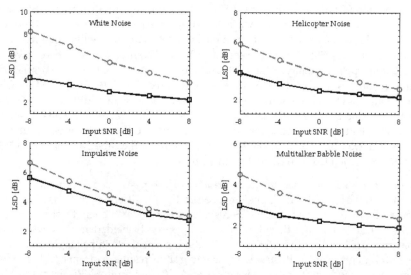

Fig. 3. Log spectral distortion measure for various noise types and levels, obtained using (○) CSS approach, and (□) the MCPSD-based method.

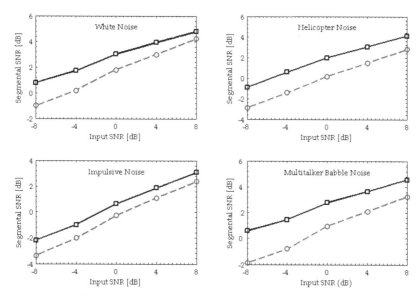

Fig. 4. Segmental SNR improvement for various noise types and levels, obtained using (○) CSS approach and (□) the MCPSD-based method.

5.2 Speech spectrograms

Objective measures alone do not provide an adequate evaluation of system performance. Speech spectrograms constitute a well-suited tool for analyzing the time-frequency behavior of any speech enhancement system. All the speech spectrograms presented in this section (Figs. 5–8) use sentence 1 corrupted with different background noises at SNR = 0 dB.

In the case of white Gaussian noise (Fig. 5), whereas the MCPSD-based method and the CSS-based approach provided sufficient amount of noise reduction, the spectrum of the former preserved better the desired speech components. In the case of helicopter rotor noise (Fig. 6), large residual noise components were observed in the spectrograms of the signals processed by the CSS-based approach. Unlike this method, the spectrogram of the signal processed by the MCPSD-based method indicated that the noise between the speech periods was noticeably reduced, while the shape of the speech periods was nearly unchanged. In the case of impulsive noise (Fig. 7), it can be observed that the CSS-based approach was less effective for this type of noise. In contrast, the spectrogram of the signal processed by the MCPSD-based method shows that the impulsive noise was moderately reduced in both the speech and noise periods. In the case of multitalker babble noise (Fig. 8), it can be seen that the CSS-based approach provided limited noise reduction, particularly in the noise only periods. By contrast, a good noise reduction was achieved by the MCPSD-based method on the entire spectrum.

We can conclude that, while the CSS-based approach afforded limited noise reduction, especially for highly nonstationary noise such as multitalker babble, the MCPSD-based method can deal efficiently with both stationary and transient noises with less spectral distortion even in severe noisy environments.

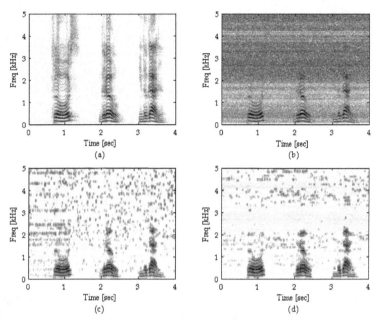

Fig. 5. Speech spectrograms obtained with white Gaussian noise added at SNR=0 dB. (a) Clean speech (b) Noisy signal (c) CSS output (d) MCPSD output.

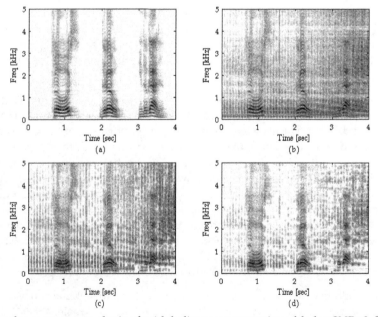

Fig. 6. Speech spectrograms obtained with helicopter rotor noise added at SNR=0 dB. (a) Clean speech (b) Noisy signal (c) CSS output (d) MCPSD output.

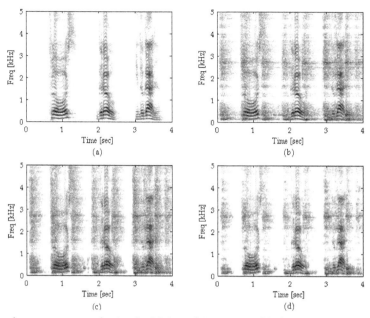

Fig. 7. Speech spectrograms obtained with impulsive noise added at SNR=0 dB. (a) Clean speech (b) Noisy signal (c) CSS output (d) MCPSD output.

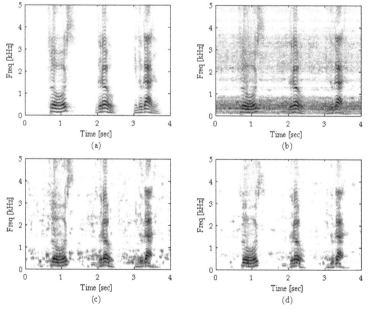

Fig. 8. Speech spectrograms obtained with multitalker babble noise added at SNR=0 dB. (a) Clean speech (b) Noisy signal (c) CSS output (d) MCPSD output.

5.3 Subjective listening tests

In order to validate the objective performance evaluation, subjective listening tests were conducted with the MCPSD and the CSS based approaches. The different noise types considered in this study were added to utterances of the five sentences listed before with SNRs of –5, 0, and 5 dB. The test signals were recorded on a portable computer, and headphones were used during the experiments. The seven-grade comparison category rating (CCR) was used (ITU-T, Recommendation P.800, 1996). The two methods were scored by a panel of twelve subjects asked to rate every sequence of two test signals between –3 and 3. A negative score was given whenever the former test signal sounded more pleasant and natural to the listener than the latter. Zero was selected if there was no difference between the two test signals. For each subject, the following procedure was applied: 1) each sequence of two test signals was played with brief pauses in between tracks and repeated twice in a random order; 2) the listener was then asked if he wished to hear the current sequence once more or skip to the next. This led to 60 scores for each test session which took about 25 minutes per subject. The results, averaged over the 12 listeners' scores and the 5 test sentences, are shown in Fig. 9. For the considered background noises, CCRs ranging from 0.33 to 1.27 were achieved over the alternative approach. The maximum improvement of CCR was obtained in the case of helicopter noise (1.1) and multitalker babble noise (1.27), while the worst score was achieved for additive white noise (0.33). The reason behind the roughly similar performance of the two methods in the case of white noise can be understood by recognizing that the minimum statistics noise PSD estimator performs better in the presence of stationary noise as opposed to nonstationary noise.

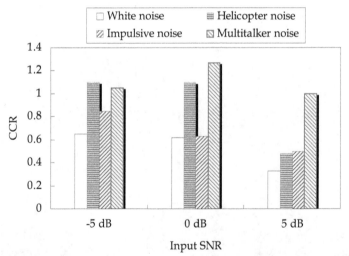

Fig. 9. CCR improvement against CSS for various noise types and different SNRs.

6. Conclusion

Given two received signals corrupted by additive noise, adding a noise power spectrum estimator after the CPSD-based noise reduction system, can substantially reduce the residual and coherent noise components that would otherwise be present at the output spectrum. The added noise power estimator seeks to provide a good tradeoff between the amount of noise reduction and the speech distortion, while attenuating the high energy correlated noise components, especially in the low frequency ranges. The performance evaluation of the modified CPSD-based method, formerly named MCPSD in this chapter, was carried out over the CSS-based approach, a dual-microphone method previously reported in the literature. Objective evaluation results show that a performance improvement in terms of segmental SNR of about 2 dB on average can be achieved by the MCPSD-based method over the CSS-based approach. The best noise reduction was obtained in the case of multitalker babble noise, while the improvement was lower for impulsive noise. Subjective listening tests performed on a limited data set revealed that CCRs ranging from 0.33 to 1.27 can be achieved over the CSS-based approach. The maximum improvement of CCR was obtained in the case of helicopter and multitalker babble noises, while the worst score was achieved when white noise was added. A fruitful direction of further research would therefore be to extend the MCPSD-based method to multiple microphones as well as to investigate the benefits of such extension on the overall system performance.

7. References

Benesty, J. et al. (2005). Speech Enhancement, Springer, ISBN 978-3540240396, New York, USA.

Berghe, J.V. & Wooters, J. (1998). An adaptive noise canceller for hearing aids using two nearby microphones. *Journal of the Acoustical Society of America*, vol. 103, no. 6, pp. 3621–3626.

Bitzer, J. et al. (1999). Theoretical noise reduction limits of the generalized sidelobe canceller (GSC) for speech enhancement. *24th IEEE International Conference on Acoustics, Speech & Signal Processing*, vol. 5, pp. 2965–2968, Phoenix, USA, March 1999.

Cohen, I. & Berdugo, B. (2002). Noise estimation by minima controlled recursive averaging for robust speech enhancement. *IEEE Transaction on Signal & Audio Processing*, vol. 9, no. 1, pp. 12–15.

Cohen, I. et al. (2003a). An integrated real-time beamforming and postfiltering system for nonstationary noise environments. *EURASIP Journal on Applied Signal Processing*, pp. 1064–1073.

Cohen, I. (2003b). Noise spectrum estimation in adverse environments: improved minima controlled recursive averaging. *IEEE Transaction on Speech & Audio Processing*, vol. 11, no. 5, pp. 466–475.

Cohen, I. (2004). Multichannel post-filtering in nonstationary noise environments. *IEEE Transaction on Signal Processing*, vol. 52, no. 5, pp. 1149–1160.

Ephraim, Y. & Malah, D. (1984). Speech enhancement using a minimum mean-square error short-time spectral amplitude estimator. *IEEE Transaction on Audio, Speech & Signal Processing*, vol. 32, no. 6, pp. 1109-1121.

Fischer, S. & Simmer, K.U. (1996). Beamforming microphone arrays for speech acquisition in noisy environments. *Speech Communication*, vol. 20, no. 3–4, pp. 215–227.

Fischer, S. & Kammeyer, K.D. (1997). Broadband beamforming with adaptive postfiltering for speech acquisition in noisy environments. *22th IEEE International Conference on Acoustics, Speech & Signal Processing*, vol. 1, pp. 359–362, Munich, Germany, April 1997.

Griffiths, L.J. & Jim, C.W. (1982). An alternative approach to linearly constrained adaptive beamforming. *IEEE Transaction on Antennas & Propagation*, vol. 30, no. 1, pp. 27–34.

Guerin, A. et al. (2003). A two-sensor noise reduction system: applications for hands-free car kit. *EURASIP Journal on Applied Signal Processing*, pp. 1125–1134.

Itakura, F. (1975). Minimum prediction residual principle applied to speech recognition. *IEEE Transaction on Audio Speech & Signal Processing*, vol. 23, pp. 67-72.

ITU-T, Recommendation P.800 (1996). Methods for subjective determination of transmission quality. *International Telecommunication Union Radiocommunication Assembly*.

Kaneda, Y. & Tohyama, M. (1984). Noise suppression signal processing using 2-point received signal. *Electronics and Communications in Japan*, vol. 67–A, pp. 19–28.

Le Bouquin-Jannès, R. et al. (1997). Enhancement of speech degraded by coherent and incoherent noise using a cross-spectral estimator. *IEEE Transaction on Speech & Audio Processing*, vol. 5, pp. 484–487.

Lefkimmiatis, S. & Maragos, P. (2007). A generalized estimation approach for linear and nonlinear microphone array post-filters. *Speech Communication*, vol. 49, pp. 657–666.

Maj, J.B. et al. (2006). Comparison of adaptive noise reduction algorithms in dual microphone hearing aids. *Speech Communication*, vol. 48, no. 8, pp. 957–970.

Marro, C. et al. (1998). Analysis of noise reduction and dereverberation techniques based on microphone arrays with postfiltering. *IEEE Transaction on Speech & Audio Processing*, vol. 6, no. 3, pp. 240–259.

Martin, R. (2001). Noise power spectral estimation based on optimal smoothing and minimum statistics. *IEEE Transaction on Signal & Audio Processing*, vol. 9, pp. 504–512.

Martin, R. (2006). Bias compensation methods for minimum statistics noise power spectral density estimation. *Signal Processing*, vol. 86, no. 6, pp. 1215–1229.

Mauler, D. & Martin, R. (2006). Noise power spectral density estimation on highly correlated data. *10th International Workshop on Acoustic, Echo & Noise Control*, Paris, France, September 2006.

McCowan, I.A. & Bourlard, H. (2003). Microphone array post-filter based on noise field coherence. *IEEE Transaction on Speech & Audio Processing*, vol. 11, no. 6, pp. 709–716.

Mittal, U. & Phamdo, N. (2000). Signal/Noise KLT based approach for enhancing speech degraded by colored noise. *IEEE Transaction on Speech & Audio Processing*, vol. 8, no. 2, pp. 159-167.

Nilsson, M. et al. (1994). Development of the hearing in noise test for the measurement of speech reception thresholds in quiet and in noise. *Journal of the Acoustical Society of America*, vol. 95, no. 2, pp. 1085-1099.

O'Shaughnessy, D. (2000). *Speech Communications, Human and Machine*, IEEE Press, ISBN 0-7803-3449-3, New York, USA.

Quakenbush, S. et al. (1988). Objective Measures of Speech Quality. Englewood Cliffs, Prentice-Hall, ISBN/ISSN 0136290566, 9780136290568.

Simmer, K.U. & Wasiljeff, A. (1992). Adaptive microphone arrays for noise suppression in the frequency domain. *Second COST229 Workshop on Adaptive Algorithms in Communications*, pp. 185–194, Bordeaux, France, October 1992.

Simmer, K.U. et al. (1994). Suppression of coherent and incoherent noise using a microphone array. *Annales des Télécommunications*, vol. 49, pp. 439–446.

Zelinski, R. (1988). A microphone array with adaptive post-filtering for noise reduction in reverberant rooms. *13th IEEE International Conference on Acoustics, Speech & Signal Processing*, vol. 5, pp. 2578–2581, NY, USA, April 1988.

Zelinski, R. (1990). Noise reduction based on microphone array with LMS adaptive post-filtering. *Electronic Letters*, vol. 26, no. 24, pp. 2036-2581.

Zhang, X. & Jia, Y. (2005). A soft decision based noise cross power spectral density estimation for two-microphone speech enhancement systems. *IEEE International Conference on Acoustics, Speech & Signal Processing*, vol. 1, pp. I/813–16, Philadelphia, USA, March 2005.

3

Multi-Resolution Spectral Analysis of Vowels in Tunisian Context

Nefissa Annabi-Elkadri, Atef Hamouda and Khaled Bsaies
URPAH Research Unit, Computer Science Department, Faculty of Sciences of Tunis.
Tunis El Manar University, Tunis
Tunisia

1. Introduction

Classic speech spectrogram shows log-magnitude amplitude (dB) versus time and frequency. The sound pressure level in dB is approximately proportional to the volume perceived by the ear. The classic speech sonagram offers a single integration time which is the length of the window. It implements a uniform bandpass filter, the spectral samples are regularly spaced and correspond to equal bandwidths. The choice of the window length determines the time-frequency resolution for all frequencies of sonagram. The more the window is narrower, the better the time resolution and the worse the frequency resolution. This implies that the display resolution of formants, voicing and frictions at low frequencies is less good than the resolution of the bursts in the high frequencies and vice versa. It is so necessary to make the right choice of windows compared to the signal.

(Mallat, 1989, p.674) remarks *"it is difficult to analyze the information content of an image directly from the gray-level intensity of the image pixels... Generally, the structures we want to recognize have very different sizes. Hence, it is not possible to define a priori an optimal resolution for analyzing images."*. To improve the standard spectral output, we can calculate a multi-resolution (MR) spectrum. In the original papers, the MR analysis is based on discrete wavelet transforms (Grossmann & Morlet, 1984; Mallat, 1989; 2000; 2008). Since that it has been applied to several domains: image analysis (Mallat, 1989), time-frequency analysis (Cnockaert, 2008), speech enhancement (Fu & Wan, 2003; Manikandan, 2006), automatic signal segmentation by search of stationary areas from the scalogram (Leman & Marque, 1998).

The MR spectrum, a compromise that provides both a higher frequency and a higher temporal resolution, is not a new method. In phonetic analysis, (Annabi-Elkadri & Hamouda, 2010; 2011) presents a study of two common vowels [a] and [E] in Tunisian dialect and french language. Vowels are pronounced in Tunisian context. The analysis of the obtained results shows that due to the influence of french language on the Tunisian dialect, the vowels [a] and [E] are, in some contexts, similarly pronounced. Annabi-Elkadri & Hamouda (2011 (in press) applies the MRS for an automatic method for Silence/Sonorant/Non-Sonorant detection used the ANOVA method. Results are compared to the classical methods for classifications such as Standard Deviation and Mean with ANOVA who were better. The method for automatic Silence/Sonorant/Non-Sonorant detection based on MRS provides better results when compared to classical spectral analysis. Cheung & Lim (1991) presented a method for combining the wideband spectrogram and the narrowband spectrogram by evaluating the geometric mean of their corresponding pixel values. The combined spectrogram appears to preserve the visual features associated with high resolution in both frequency and time. Lee & Ching (1999) described an approach of using multi-resolution analysis (MRA) for clean connected speech and noisy phone conversation speech. Experiments show that the use of MRA cepstra results reduces significantly error insertion when compared with MFCCs. For music signals, Cancela et al. (2009) presents two algorithms: efficient constant-Q transform and multi-resolution FFT. They are reviewed and compared with a new proposal based on the IIR filtering of the FFT. The proposed method shows to be a good compromise between design flexibility and reduced computational effort. Additionally, it was used as a part of an effective melody extraction algorithm. In this context, Dressler was interested in the description of spectral analysis to extract melodies based on spectrograms multi-resolution (Dressler, 2006). The approach aims to extract the sinusoidal components of the audio signal. A calculation of the spectra of different resolutions of frequencies is done in order to detect sinusoids stable in different frames of the FFT. The evaluated results showed that the multi-resolution analysis improves the extraction of the sinusoidal.

The aim of this study was an extension of Annabi-Elkadri & Hamouda (2010; 2011) researches. We presented and tested the concept of multi-resolution for the spectral analysis (MRS) of vowels in Tunisian words and in French words under the Tunisian context. Our method was composed of two parts. The first part was applied MRS method to the signal. MRS was calculated by combining several FFT of different lengths (Annabi-Elkadri & Hamouda, 2010; 2011). The second part was the formant detection by applied multi-resolution LPC (Annabi-Elkadri & Hamouda, 2010). We present an improvement of our method of multi-resolution spectral analysis MR FFT. As an application, we used our system VASP for a Tunisian Dialect corpus pronounced by Tunisian speakers.

Standard Arabic is composed by 34 phonemes (Muhammad, 1990). It has three vowels, with long and short forms of [a], [i], and [u]. Arabic phonemes are classified in two classes pharyngeal and emphatic. There are characteristics of semitic languages (Elshafei, 1991; Muhammad, 1990). Arabic has two kinds of syllables: open syllables (CV) and (CVV) and closed syllables (CVC), (CVVC), and (CVCC). Syllables (CVVC) and (CVCC) occur only at the end of the sentence. V is a vowel and C is a consonant (Muhammad, 1990).

In section 2, we presented a brief history of Tunisian Dialect and it's relationship with Arabic and French. In section 3, we presented our calculated method of the multi-resolution FFT. In section 4, we presented the materials and methods composed by our corpus and our system Visual Assistance of Speech Processing Software (VASP). We presented our experimental results in section 5 and we discussed it in section 6. Our conclusion is presented in section 7.

2. History of Tunisian dialect and it's relationship with Arabic and French

The official language in Tunisia is Arabic. But, the popular language is the Tunisian Dialect (TD). It is a mix of Arabic with a lot of other languages: French, Italian, English, Turkich, German, Berber and Spanish. This mixture is related to the history of Tunisia, since it was invaded and colonized by many civilizations like the Romans, Vandals, Byzantains, the Arab Moslems and French.

After French colonization, the French government wanted to spread the French language in the country. The French instituted a bilingual education system with the Franco-Arab schools. Programs of bilingual schools were modeled primarily on the model of French primary education for children of European origin (French, Italian and Maltese), which were added courses in colloquial Arabic. As for the Tunisian children, they received their education in classical Arabic in order to study the Quoran. Only a small Tunisian elite received a truly bilingual education, in order to co-administer the country. Tunisian Muslim mass continued to speak only Arabic or one of its many varieties. The report of the Tunisian Minister of Affairs, Jean-Jules Jusserand, pursuing the logic of Jules Ferry. In a "Note on Education in Tunisia", dated February 1882, Jusserand exposing his ideas: *"We have not at this time we better way to assimilate the Arabs of Tunisia, to the extent that is possible, that they learn our language, it is the opinion of all who know them best: we can not rely on religion to make this comparison, they do not convert to Christianity, but as they learn our language, a host of European ideas will prove to be bound to them, as experience has sufficiently demonstrated. In the reorganization of Tunisia, a large part must be made to education"*.

After independence, education of the French language such as Arabic was required for all Tunisian children in primary school. This explains why French has become the second language in Tunisia. It is spoken by the majority of the population.

There are different varieties of TD depending on the region, such as dialect of Tunis, Sahel, Sfax, etc. Its morphology, syntax, pronunciation and vocabulary are quite different from the Arabic (Marcais, 1950). There are several differences in pronunciation between Standard Arabic and TD. Short vowels are frequently omitted, especially where they would occur as the final element of an open syllable. While Standard Arabic can have only one consonant at the beginning of a syllable, after which a vowel must follow, TD commonly has two consonants in the onset. For example Standard Arabic "book" is /kita?b/, while in TD, it is /kta?b/. The nucleus in TD may contain a short or long vowel, and at the end of the syllable, in the coda, it may have up to three consonants, but in standard Arabic, we cannot have more than two consonants at the end of the syllable. Word-internal syllables are generally heavy in that they either have a long vowel in the nucleus or consonant in the coda. Non-final syllables composed of just a consonant and a short vowel (i.e. light syllables) are very rare in TD, and are generally loaned from standard Arabic: short vowels in this position have generally been lost, resulting in the many initial CC clusters. For example /?awa?b/ "reply" is a loan from Standard Arabic, but the same word has the natural development /?wa?b/, which is the usual word for "letter" (Gibson, 1998).

In TD's non-pharyngealised context, there is a strong fronting and closing of /a?/, which, especially among younger speakers in Tunis can reach as far as /e?/, and to a lesser extent of /a/.

This is an example of Tunisian Arabic sentence (SAMPA and X-SAMPA symbols): '/ddZ   bA : k   Ukil ?\adailkas mta?\u   milEna bil   lE   sykse/'. This sentence is a mixture of three languages; '/ddZ   bA : k/' in English, '/Ukil   ?\ada   ilkas   mta?\u milEna   bil/' in Tunisian Arabic, which means *'as usual the show is interesting'* and finally '/lE   sykse/' in French, which means *'success'*.

We introduce a study of six common vowels [a], [E], [i], [e], [o] and [u] in TD and French. Vowels are pronounced in Tunisian context. Our study is realized in time-frequency domain.

3. Multi-resolution FFT

It's so difficult to choose the ideal window with the ideal characteristics. The size of the ideal window (Hancq & Leich, 2000) was equal to twice the length of the pitch of the signal. A wider window show the harmonics in the spectrum, a shorter window approximated very roughly the spectral envelope. This amounts to estimate the energy dispersion with the least error. When we calculated the windowed FFT, we supposed that the eneregy was concentrated at the center of the frame (Haton & al., 2006, p.41). We noted the center C_p. So our problem now, is the estimation of C_p.

3.1 The center estimation in the case of the Discrete Fourier Transform (DFT)

We would like to calculate the spectral of the speech signal s. We note L the length of s. The first step is to sample s into frames. The size of each frame was between 10 ms and 20 ms (Calliope, 1989; Ladefoged, 1996) to meet the stationnarity condition. We choosed the Hamming window and we fixed the size to 512 points and the overlap to 50%. Figure 1 shows the principle of the center estimation.

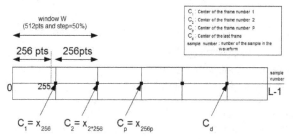

Fig. 1. Signal sampling and windowing for center estimation C_p. The window length $N = 512$ points and overlap = 50%.

For each frame p, the center C_p was estimated:

$$\begin{cases} C_1 = x_{256} & for \quad p = 1 \\ C_2 = x_{2*256} & for \quad p = 2 \\ \quad \vdots \\ C_p = x_{256p} & in \quad general \quad case \end{cases}$$

The center $C_p = x_{256p}$ with $p = 1...[\frac{L-1}{256} - 1]$ and $[\ \ ]$ the integer part.

Each signal s was sampled into frames. Each frame number p was composed by $N = 512$ points:

$$\begin{cases} s_0(p) = x_{256(p-1)} \\ s_1(p) = x_{256(p-1)+1} \\ \quad \vdots \\ s_{511}(p) = x_{256(p-1)+511} \end{cases}$$

In general case, for the componant number l of s:

$$s_l(p) = x_{256(p-1)+l}$$

The FFT windowing for the frame number p was calculated as:

$$S_k(p) = \sum_{l=0}^{511} s_l(p)e^{-\frac{2j\pi kl}{512}} w(s_l(p) - s_{256}(p)) \tag{1}$$

In general case:

$$S_k(p) = \sum_{l=0}^{N-1} s_l(p)e^{-\frac{2j\pi kl}{N}} w(s_l(p) - s_{\frac{N}{2}}(p)) \tag{2}$$

We noted $C_p = s_{\frac{N}{2}}(p)$ the center of the frame number p with $p = 1...[\frac{2(L-1)}{N} - 1]$, [ ] the integer part and :

$s_l(p)$: the componant of s number l of the frame p
$S_k(p)$: the componant of S number k of the frame p
L: the length of the signal s
N: the length of the window w

3.2 The center estimation in the case of the MR FFT

To improve the standard spectral, we calculated the MR FFT by combining several FFT of different lengths. The temporal accuracy is higher in the high frequency region and the resolution of high frequency in the low frequencies.

We calculated the FFT windowing of the signal several times NB. The number of steps NB was equal to the number of band frequency fixed a priori. For each step number i ($i \leq NB$), the signal s was sampled into frames $s_i(p_i)$ and windowed with the window w. We noted N_i the length of frames and of w for each step i. C_{i,p_i} was the center of w.

The spectral $S_{i,k}(p_i)$ for each step i was:

$$S_{i,k}(p_i) = \sum_{l=0}^{N_i-1} s_{i,l}(p_i)e^{-\frac{2j\pi kl}{N}} w(s_{i,l}(p_i) - C_{i,p_i}) \tag{3}$$

with: $C_{i,p_i} = s_{i,\frac{N_i}{2}}(p_i)$ the center of the frame p_i when the overlap$=\frac{N_i}{2}$.

In MRS, the overlap $\frac{N_i}{2}$ can not satisfy the principle of continuity of the MRS in different band frequencies. A low overlap causes a discontinuity in the spectrum MRS and thus give us a bad estimation of the energy dispersal. So our problem consisted on the overlap choosing. It was necessary that the frames overlap with a percentage higher to 50% of the frame length. We choosed an overlap equal to 75% (fig. 2).

For the frame $p_i = 1$ of the step number i, we have N_i components:

$$\begin{cases} s_0(1) &= x_0 \\ s_1(1) &= x_1 \\ &\vdots \\ s_l(1) &= x_l \\ &\vdots \\ s_{N_i-1}(1) &= x_{N-1} \end{cases}$$

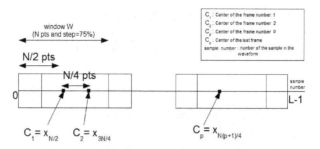

Fig. 2. Signal sampling and windowing for center estimation C_{i,p_i} (overlap = 75%).

For the frame $p_i = 2$ of the step number i, we have N_i components:

$$\begin{cases} s_0(2) &= x_{N_i} \\ s_1(2) &= x_{N_i}+1 \\ &\vdots \\ s_l(2) &= x_{N_i}+l \\ &\vdots \\ s_{N_i-1}(2) &= x_{N_i}+N_i-1 \end{cases}$$

In general case, for the frame p_i of the step number i, we have N_i components:

$$\begin{cases} s_0(p_i) &= x_{(p_i-1)N_i} \\ s_1(p_i) &= x_{(p_i-1)N_i}+1 \\ &\vdots \\ s_l(p_i) &= x_{(p_i-1)N_i}+l \\ &\vdots \\ s_{N_i-1}(p_i) &= x_{(p_i-1)N_i}+N_i-1 \\ s_{N_i-1}(p_i) &= x_{p_iN_i}-1 \end{cases}$$

The center C_{i,p_i} of $p_i = 1$ was:

$$C_{i,1} = \frac{N_i}{2}$$

The center C_{i,p_i} of $p_i = 2$ was:

$$\begin{cases} C_{i,2} &= \frac{1}{2}(\frac{1}{4}+\frac{5}{4})N_i \\ &= \frac{3}{4}N_i \end{cases}$$

In general case, the center C_{i,p_i} of p_i was:

$$\begin{cases} C_{i,p_i} &= C_{i,p_i-1}+\frac{N_i}{4} \\ &= C_{i,1}+(p_i-1)\frac{N_i}{4} \\ &= x_{\frac{N_i(p_i+1)}{4}} \end{cases}$$

with : $\frac{N_i(p_i+1)}{4} \leq L$ and $p_i \leq \frac{4L}{N_i} - 1$

The spectral $S_{i,k}(p_i)$ of each step i was :

$$S_{i,k}(p_i) = \sum_{l=0}^{N_i-1} s_{i,l}(p_i)e^{-\frac{2j\pi kl}{N}}w(s_{i,l}(p_i) - C_{i,p_i}) \tag{4}$$

with: $C_{i,p_i} = x_{\frac{N_i(p_i+1)}{4}}$ the center of the frame p_i and the overlap equal to 75%.

So, the multi-resolution spectral MRS was:

$$S_k(p) = S_{i,k}(p_i)sik_i \leq k \leq k_{i+1} \tag{5}$$

with: $0 \leq k \leq N_0 + N_1 + \ldots + N_P$ and $1 \leq p \leq P$.

The size of the ideal window (Hancq & Leich, 2000) is equal to twice the length of the pitch of the signal. A wider window shows the harmonics in the spectrum, a shorter window approximates very roughly the spectral envelope.

To improve the standard spectral, we calculate a multi-resolution spectral (MRS) with two methods; by combining several FFT of different lengths and by combining several windows for each FFT (Annabi-Elkadri & Hamouda, 2010).

Diagrams displayed in figure 3 illustrates the difference between the standard FFT and the MRS. For a standard FFT, the size of the window is equal for each frequency band unlike the MRS windows size. It is dependent on the frequency band.

Fig. 3. Standard FFT (on the left) and MR FFT (on the right)

Figure 4 shows the classical sonagram; Hamming window, 11 ms with an overlap equal to 1/3. The sentence pronounced is: "Le soir approchait, le soir du dernier jour de l'anné". Figure 5 shows the multi-resolution sonagram of the same sentence. It offers several time integrations which are combinations of several FFT of different lengths depending on frequency bandwidth.

4. Materials and methods

4.1 Corpus

Our corpus is composed of TD prounounced by Tunisian speakers. The sampling frequency is equal to 44.1 KHz, the wav format was adopted in mono-stereo. We avoided all types

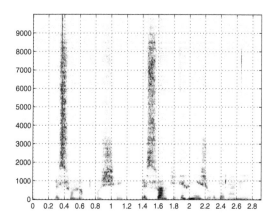

Fig. 4. Classical sonagram (Hamming, 11 ms, overlap 1/3) of this sentence: "Le soir approchait, le soir du dernier jour de l'année"

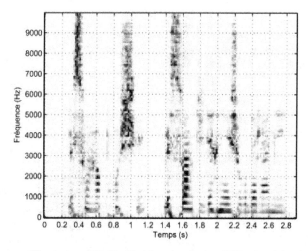

Fig. 5. MR sonagram; Hamming (23, 20, 15, 11 ms), overlap 75%, Band-limits in Hz were [0, 2000, 4000, 7000, 10000] of this sentence: "Le soir approchait, le soir du dernier jour de l'année"

of noise filter that would degrade the quality of the signal and thus, causes information lost. We have recorded a real time spontaneous lyrics and discussions of 4 speakers. We have removed noise and funds sounds like laughing, music, etc. It was difficult to realize a spontaneous corpus because, in real time, it is impossible to have all phonemes and syllables. Another difficulty was the variability of discussion themes and pronounced sounds. For these reasons, we decided to complete our corpus with another one. We prepared a text in Tunisian dialect with all sounds to study. Every phoneme and syllable appeared 15 times. We asked from four speakers: two men and two women, to read the text in a high voice in the same conditions of the first corpus records. All speakers are between 25 and 32 years old.

Speakers don't know the text. The sampling frequency is equal to 44,1 KHz, the wav format was adopted in mono-stereo. We avoided the remarkable accents and all types of noise filter that would degrade the quality of the signal and thus, causes information lost. Our corpus was transcribed in sentences, words and phonemes.

4.2 VASP software: Visual assistance of speech processing software

For our study, we have created our first prototype System for Visual Assistance of Speech Processing VASP. It offers many functions for speech visualization and analysis. We developed our system with GUI Matlab. In the following subsection, we will present some of the functionalities offered by our system.

VASP reads sound files in wav format. It represent a wav file in time domain by waveform and in time-frequency domain by spectral representation, classical spectrogram in narrow band and wide band (see figure 6), spectrograms calculated with linear prediction and cepstral coefficients, gammatone, discrete cosine transform (DCT), Wigner-Ville transformation, multi-resolution LPC representation (MR LPC), multi-resolution spectral representation (MR FFT) and multi-resolution spectrogram.

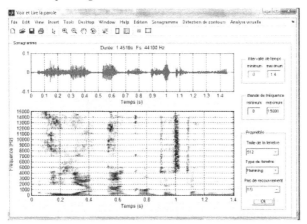

Fig. 6. Classical Spectrogram Interface.

From waveform, we can choose, in real time, the frame for which we want to represent a spectrum (see figure 7). Parameters are manipulated from a menu; we can select the type of windows (Hamming, Hanning, triangular, rectangular, Kaiser, Barlett, gaussian and Blackmann-Harris), window length (64, 128, 256, 512, 1024 and 2048 samples) and LPC factor.

From all visual representations, coordinates of any pixel can be read. For example, we can select a point from a spectrogram and read its coordinates directly (time, frequency and intensity).

VASP offers the possibility to choose a part of a signal to calculate and visualize it in any time-frequency representations.

Our system can automatically detect Silence/Speech from a waveform. From the spectrogram, the system can detect acoustic cues like formants, and classify it automatically to two classes: sonorant or non-sonorant.

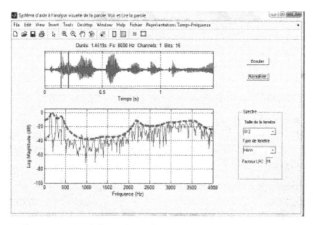

Fig. 7. Waveform and spectrum of the selected signal.

Our system can analyse visual representations with two methods image analysis with edge detection and sound analysis signal. Edge detection is calculated with gradiant method or median filter method (fig.8). The second method is based on detecting energy from a time-frequency representation.

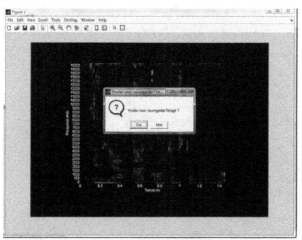

Fig. 8. Edge detection calculated with the gradiant method.

5. Experimental results

Formants frequencies are the properties of the vocal tract system and need to be inferred from the speech signal rather than just measured. The spectral shape of the vocal tract excitation strongly influences the observed spectral envelope. However, not all vocal tract resonances can cause peaks in the observed spectral envelope.

To extract formants frequencies from the signal, we resampled it to 8 KHz. We use a linear prediction method for our analysis. Linear prediction models the signal as if it were generated by a signal of minimum energy being passed through a purely-recursive IIR filter. Multi-resolution LPC (MR LPC) is calculated by the LPC of the average of the convolution of several windows to the signal.

To our knowledge, there is no normative studies in Standard Arabic vowels like those of Peterson and Barney (Peterson & Barney, 1952) for American english, and those of Fant and al. (Fant, 1969) for Swedish.

We applied VASP on TD and French language. We measured the two first formants F1 and F2 of vowels in Tunisian and French words. We compared our experimental results with those for Calliope (Calliope, 1989). Their corpus is constituted of vowels repetitions in [p_R] context and pronounced by 10 men and 9 women.

The analysis of the obtained results shows that due to the influence of French language on the TD, the vowels [a], [E], [i], [e], [o] and [u] are, in some contexts, similarly pronounced.

5.1 Tunisian dialect and French spectral analysis of [a] in Tunisian context

We measured the two first formants F1 and F2 of vowels [a] in Tunisian and french words in Tunisian context. Figures 9(a) and 9(b) show scatters of formants respectively for [a] in Tunisian words and in french words. There was a high matching of the two scatters for F1 (400-700 Hz) and for F2 (500-3000 Hz).

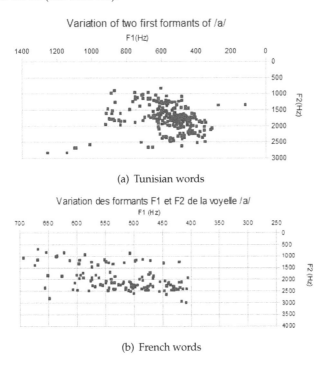

(a) Tunisian words

(b) French words

Fig. 9. Variation of two first formants of [a].

5.2 Tunisian dialect and French spectral analysis of [E] in Tunisian context

We measured the two first formants F1 and F2 of vowels [E] in Tunisian and french words in Tunisian context. Figures 10(a) and 10(b) show scatters of formants respectively for [E] in Tunisian words and in french words. There is a high matching of the two scatters for F1 (300-550 Hz) and for F2 (1500-3000 Hz).

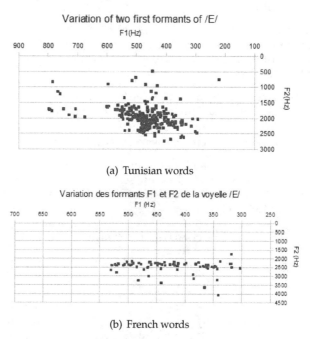

(a) Tunisian words

(b) French words

Fig. 10. Variation of two first formants of [E].

5.3 Tunisian dialect and French spectral analysis of [i] in Tunisian context

We measured the two first formants F1 and F2 of vowels [i] in Tunisian and french words in Tunisian context. Figures 11(a) and 11(b) show scatters of formants respectively for [i] in Tunisian words and in french words. There is a high matching of the two scatters for F1 (250-400 Hz) and for F2 (1800-2500 Hz).

5.4 Tunisian dialect spectral analysis of [o] and [e] in Tunisian context

We measured the two first formants F1 and F2 of vowels [o] and [e] in Tunisian words. Figure 12(a) and 12(b) show scatters of formants for [o] and [e] in Tunisian words.

5.5 Tunisian dialect and French spectral analysis of [u] in Tunisian context

We measured the two first formants F1 and F2 of vowels [u] in Tunisian and french words in Tunisian context. Figures 13(a) and 13(b) show scatters of formants respectively for [u] in Tunisian words and in french words. There is a high matching of the two scatters for F1 (300-440 Hz) and for F2 (1500-3000 Hz).

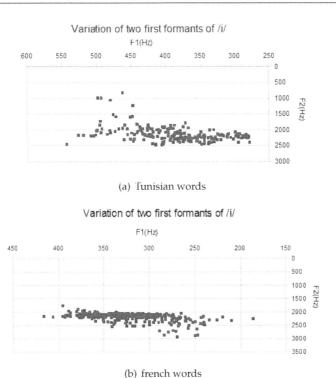

(a) Tunisian words

(b) french words

Fig. 11. Variation of two first formants of [i].

5.6 Results of Tunisian dialect formants variation

Figure 14 show scatters of formants mean for vowels [a], [e], [E], [o], [i] and [u] in Tunisian words.

6. Discussion

We compared our experimental results with those for Calliope (1989) in tables 1, 2, 3, 4 and 5. Their corpus was constituted of two repetitions of [a], [E], [i], [o], [e] and [u] in [p_R] context and pronounced by 10 men and 9 women.

	Calliope		French		Tunisian Dialect	
	F1	F2	F1	F2	F1	F2
Med	684	1256	512	2137	515	1758
SD	47	32	74	600	158	383

Table 1. Values of median (Med) and Standard Deviation (SD) of two first formants (F1, F2) of [a] for Tunisian Dialect and French language

In French, [i] was a front vowel. The difference between the two first formants was great. F1 was around 200 Hz and F2 was greater than 2000 Hz. For the Tunisian dialect, we note that

Variation of two first formants of /o/

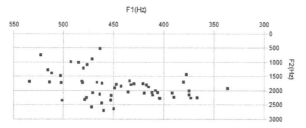

(a) Variation of two first formants of [o]

Variation of two first formants of /e/

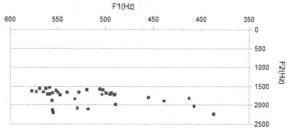

(b) Variation of two first formants of [e]

Fig. 12. Variation of two first formants of [o] and [e] for Tunisian words.

	Calliope		French		Tunisian Dialect	
	F1	F2	F1	F2	F1	F2
Med	530	1718	436	2374	464	2017
SD	49	132	63	354	90	360

Table 2. Values of median (Med) and Standard Deviation (SD) of two first formants (F1, F2) of [E] for Tunisian Dialect and French language

	Calliope		French		Tunisian Dialect	
	F1	F2	F1	F2	F1	F2
Med	308	2064	307.69	2175.12	384.3	2181.32
SD	34	134	415.37	241.61	61.57	249.6

Table 3. Values of median (Med) and Standard Deviation (SD) of two first formants (F1, F2) of [i] for Tunisian Dialect and French language

the [i] retains the characteristic of front vowel. The average value of F1 was 443 Hz, more higher than that of the French language. It can be considered as a lax variant of the vowel [i]. It was like close-mid front vowel. The tongue was positioned halfway between a close vowel and a mid vowel but it was less constricted.

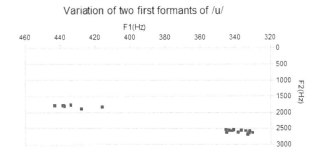

(a) Tunisian words

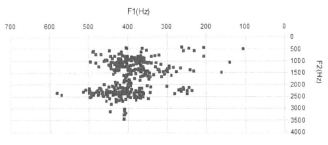

(b) french words

Fig. 13. Variation of two first formants of [u].

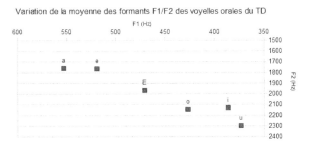

Fig. 14. Variation of two first formants of Tunisian Dialect Vowels.

	[o] for Calliope		[e] for Calliope		[o] for Tunisian Dialect		[e] for Tunisian Dialect	
	F1	F2	F1	F2	F1	F2	F1	F2
Med	383	793	381	1417	381.4	2184.32	380.23	2188.11
SD	22	63	44	106	37.88	258.24	39.85	153.44

Table 4. Values of median (Med) and Standard Deviation (SD) of two first formants (F1, F2) of [e] and [o] for Tunisian Dialect and French language

	Calliope		French		Tunisian Dialect	
	F1	F2	F1	F2	F1	F2
Med	315	764	575.52	2355.61	381.58	2183.57
SD	43	59	199.38	172.25	48.05	392.42

Table 5. Values of median (Med) and Standard Deviation (SD) of two first formants (F1, F2) of [u] for Tunisian Dialect and French language

We can say the same thing about [u] for Tunisian dialect. The average value of F1, equal to 406 Hz, was greater than that of the French language (200 Hz) and the average value of F2, equal to 2195 Hz, was higher than that of the French language (1200 Hz).

The vowel [a] was open front. The average value of F1 was equal to 443 Hz and the average value of F2 was equal to 2090 Hz for Tunisian dialect. F1 was less than the average of first French formant (700 Hz). F2 takes a greater value than the average second French formant (1500 Hz). Therefore, we can say that the position of the tongue was narrower and it was positioned as far forward as possible in the mouth for the Tunisian dialect.

In opposition to all vowels studied, the [E] of the Tunisian dialect was same to the [E] of the French language. We note an average of 436 Hz for F1 and 2120 Hz for F2.

For the vowels [a] and [E] the F1 median was nearer to Calliope for TD than for French language. For TD and French language, the F1 medians are far from Calliope for F2 median but near each other. For the vowel [E], the F1 and F2 Standard Deviation was high and far from Calliope for TD and French language. This may be explained by the facts that the position of the tongue was narrower and it was positioned as far forward as possible in the mouth for the Tunisian dialect. High Standard Deviation was related to the small size of our corpus.

We remarked that Tunisian speakers pronounce vowels in the same way for both French language and TD.

7. Conclusion

The analysis of the obtained results shows that due to the influence of French language on the Tunisian dialect, the vowels are, in some contexts, similarly pronounced. It will be interesting to extend the study to other vowels, on a large corpus and to compare it with the study of other languages corpus like Standard Arabic, Berber, Italian, English and Spanish.

8. References

Annabi-Elkadri, N. & Hamouda, A. (2010). Spectral analysis of vowels /a/ and /E/ in tunisian context, *2010 International Conference on Audio, Language and Image Processing*, number CFP1050D-ART in *978-1-4244-5858-5*, IEEE/IET indexed in both EI and ISTP. (in Press).

Annabi-Elkadri, N. & Hamouda, A. (2011). Analyse spectrale des voyelles /a/ et /E/ dans le contexte tunisien, *Actes des IXe Rencontres des Jeunes Chercheurs en Parole RJCP*, Université Stendhal, Grenoble, pp. 1–4.

Annabi-Elkadri, N. & Hamouda, A. (2011 (in press)). Automatic Silence/ Sonorant/ Non-Sonorant Detection based on Multi-resolution Spectral Analysis and ANOVA

Method, *International Workshop on Future Communication and Networking*, IEEE, Hong Kong.

Calliope (1989). *La parole et son traitement automatique*, collection technique et scientifique des télécommunications, MASSON et CENT-ENST, Paris, ISBN :2-225-81516-X, ISSN : 0221-2579.

Cancela, P., Rocamora, M. & Lopez, E. (2009). An efficient multi-resolution spectral transform for music analysis, *10th International Society for Music Information Retrieval Conference (ISMIR 2009)*, pp. 309–314.

Cheung, S. & Lim, J. (1991).   Combined multi-resolution (wideband/narrowband) spectrogram, *International Conference on Acoustics, Speech, and Signal Processing, ICASSP-91*, IEEE, pp. 457–460.

Cnockaert, L. (2008). *Analysis of vocal tremor and application to parkinsonian speakers / Analyse du tremblement vocal et application à des locuteurs parkinsoniens*, PhD thesis, F512 - Faculté des sciences appliquées - Electronique.

Dressler, K. (2006).   Sinusoidal extraction using an efficient implementation of a multi-resolution FFT, *Proceeding of the 9th International Conference on Digital Audio Effects (DAFx-06)*, pp. 247–252.

Elshafei, M. (1991).   Toward an arabic text-to-speech system, *The Arabian J. Science and Engineering*, Vol. 4B, pp. 565–583.

Fant, G. (1969). Stops in cv syllables, *STL-QPSR*, Vol. 4, pp. 1–25.

Fu, Q. & Wan, E. A. (2003). A novel speech enhancement system based on wavelet denoising, *Center of Spoken Language Understanding, OGI School of Science and Engineering at OHSU* .: .

Gibson, M. (1998). *Dialect Contact in Tunisian Arabic: sociolinguistic and structural aspects*, PhD thesis, University of Reading.

Grossmann, A. & Morlet, J. (1984). Decomposition of hardy functions into square integrable wavelets of consonant shape, *SIAM Journal on Mathematical Analysis* 15(4): 723–736.

Hancq, R. B. H. B. T. D. J. & Leich, H. (2000). *Traitement de la parole*, Presses Polytechniques et Universitaires Romandes. ISBN 2-88074-388-5.

Haton, J. & al. (2006). *Reconnaissance automatique de la parole*, DUNOD.

Ladefoged, P. (1996). *Elements of Acoustic Phonetics*, The University of Chicago Press.

Lee, C. C. Y. W. T. & Ching, P. (1999). Two-dimensional multi-resolution analysis of speech signals and its application to speech recognition, *International Conference on Acoustics, Speech, and Signal Processing, ICASSP99*, Vol. 1, IEEE, pp. 405–408.

Leman, H. & Marque, C. (1998).   Un algorithme rapide d'extraction d'arêtes dans le scalogramme et son utilisation dans la recherche de zones stationnaires / a fast ridge extraction algorithm from the scalogram, applied to search of stationary areas, *Traitement du Signal* 15(6): 577–581.

Mallat, S. (1989).   A theory for multiresolution signal decomposition : the wavelet representation, *IEEE Transaction on Pattern Analysis and Machine Intelligence* 11: 674–693.

Mallat, S. (2000). *Une Exploration des Signaux en Ondelettes*, Editions de l'Ecole Polytechnique, Ellipses diffusion.

Mallat, S. (2008). *A wavelet Tour of Signal Processing*, 3rd edition edn, Academic Press.

Manikandan, S. (2006).   Speech enhancement based on wavelet denoising, *Academic Open Internet Journal* 17(1311–4360): .

Marcais, W. (1950). *Les parlers arabes, Initiation à la Tunisie*, d. Adrien Maisonneuve, Paris.

Muhammad, A. (1990). *Alaswaat Alaghawaiyah, (in Arabic)*, Daar Alfalah, Jordan.
Peterson, G. & Barney, H. (1952). Control methods used in a study of the words, *Journal of Acoustical Society of America, JASA* 24: 175–184.

4

Mathematical Modeling of Speech Production and Its Application to Noise Cancellation

N. R. Raajan[1], T. R. Sivaramakrishnan[1] and Y. Venkatramani[2]
[1]School of Electrical and Elcetronics Engineering, SASTRA University, Thanjore
[2]Saranathan College of Engineering, Trichy
India

1. Introduction

Sound emanates by three processes, they are twisting of nerves, wires beating of membranes or blowing of air through holes. But human voice mechanism is different as it comes out in different languages and feelings by a control mechanism, the brain. As per Indian thought The soul (Atma) associates with (budhi) brain , and later inturn orders the (manas) heart. Thus the (manas) heart under the influence of (bhudhi) brain stimulates the (jathagani) simulator. The Jathagani stimulates Udanda vata and finally the (intuition) udana vata produces speech. The voice with which we speak has two components namely **1)Dhwanyaatmaka sabdas 2)VarNaatmaka sabdas**.

Dhwanyaatmaka sabdas (fricative sound)are produced as sounds without modification. These sounds are modified after they come out of the vocal cords into pharynx and mouth. Here by different types of movements in pharynx, palate, tounge checks and lips, various syllables and words are produced. the production of speech will be effected by the action of the areas of cerebral cortex viz, 1) Audio sensory, 2) Audio Psychic and 3) Audio-motor. Simply, **Dhvanyaatmaka** (fricative sound), for example, is the sound produced by the beat of a drum or the ringing of a bell, etc. **VarNaatmaka** (Plosive sound) is the sound produced by the vocal organs, namely, the throat, palate etc. For example, the sound of the letter, ka, kha, etc.

dhvani visheSasahakrta kanThataalva |
bhighaata janyashca varNaatmaka ||
shabdaartha Ratnaakara ||

Block diagram shows the complete process of producing and perceiving speech from the formulation of a message in the brain of a talker, to the creation of the speech signal, and finally to the understanding of the message by a listener. In their classic introduction to speech science. The process starts in the upper left as a message represented somehow in the brain of the speaker. The message information can be thought of as having a number of different representations during the process of speech production.

For example the message could be represented initially as English text. In order to *speak* the message, the talker implicitly converts the text into a symbolic representation of the sequence

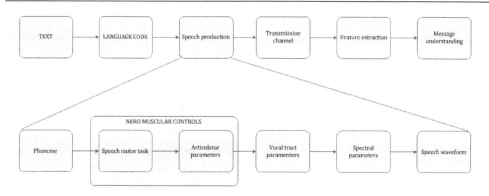

Fig. 1. Block Diagram

of sounds corresponding to the spoken version of the text. This step, called the language code generator (it is done under bhudhi (brain) converts text to speech)in Block digaram, converts text symbols to phonetic symbols (along with stress and durational information) that describe the basic sounds of a spoken version of the message and the manner (i.e., the speed and emphasis) in which the sounds are intended to be produced. As there are labeled with phonetic symbols using a computer-keyboard-friendly code called ARPAbet. Thus, the text *shouldwechase* is represented phonetically (in ARPAbet symbols) as [SH UH D W IY CH EY S]. The third step in the speech production process is the conversion to *neuromuscularcontrols*, i.e., the set of control signals that direct the neuromuscular system to move the speech articulators, namely the tongue, lips, teeth,jaw and velum, in a manner that is consistent with the sounds of the desired spoken message and with the desired degree of emphasis. The end result of the neuromuscular controls step is a set of articulatory motions (continuous control) that cause the vocal tract articulators to move in a prescribed manner in order to create the desired sounds. Finally the last step in the Speech Production process is the *vocaltractsystem* that physically creates the necessary sound sources and the appropriate vocal tract shapes over time so as to create an acoustic waveform, that encodes the information in the desired message into the speech signal. To determine the rate of information flow during speech production, assume that there are about 32 symbols (letters) in the language(in English there are 26 letters, but if we include simple punctuation. we get a count closer to 32 = 2^5symbols). Furthermore, the rate of speaking for most people is about 10 symbols per second (somewhat on the high side, but still acceptable for a rough information rate estimate). Hence, assuming independent letters as a simple approximation, we estimate the base information rate of the text message as about 50 bps (5 bits per symbol times 10 symbols per second). At the second stage of the process, where the text representation is converted into phonemes and prosody (e.g., pitch and stress) markers, the information rate is estimated to increase by a factor of 4 to about 200 bps. For example, the ARBAbet phonetic symbol set used to label the speech sounds contains approximately 64 = 2^6 symbols, or about 6 bits/phoneme (again a rough approximation assuming independence of phonemes). There are 8 phonemes in approximately 600ms. This leads to an estimate of 8 Œ 6/0.6 = 80 bps. Additional information required to describe prosodic features of the signal (e.g., duration, pitch, loudness) could easily add 100 bps to the total information rate for a message encoded as a speech signal.

The information representations for the first two stages in the speech signal are discrete so we can readily estimate the rate of information flow with some simple assumptions. For the next stage in the speech production part of the speech chain, the representation becomes continuous (in the form of control signals for articulatory motion). If they could be measured, we could estimate the spectral bandwidth of these control signals and appropriately sample and quantize these signals to obtain equivalent digital signals for which the data rate could be estimated. The articulators move relatively slowly compared to the time variation of the resulting acoustic waveform. Estimates of bandwidth and required accuracy suggest that the total data rate of the sampled articulatory control signals is about 2000 bps. Thus, the original text message is represented by a set of continuously varying signals whose digital representation requires a much higher data rate than the information rate that we estimated for transmission of the message as a speech signal.

Finally, as we will see later, the data rate of the digitized speech waveform at the end of the speech production part of the speech chain can be anywhere from 64,000 to more than 700,000 bps. We arrive at such numbers by examining the sampling rate and quantization required to represent the speech signal with a desired perceptual fidelity. For example, *telephonequality* requires that a bandwidth of 0 to 4 kHz be preserved, implying a sampling rate of 8000 samples/sec. Each sample can be quantized with 8 bits on a log scale, resulting in a bit rate of 64,000 bps. This representation is highly intelligible (i.e., humans can readily extract the message from it) but to most listeners, it will sound different from the original speech signal uttered by the talker. On the other hand, the speech waveform can be represented with *CDquality* using a sampling rate of 44,100 samples/s with 16 bit samples, or a data rate of 705,600 bps. In this case, the reproduced acoustic signal will be virtually indistinguishable from the original speech signal. As we move from text to speech waveform through the speech chain, the result is an encoding of the message that can be effectively transmitted by acoustic wave propagation and robustly decoded by the hearing mechanism of a listener. The above analysis of data rates shows that as we move from text to sampled speech waveform, the data rate can increase by a factor of 10,000. Part of this extra information represents characteristics of the talker such as emotional state, speech mannerisms, accent, etc., but much of it is due to the inefficiency of simply sampling and finely quantizing analog signals. Thus, motivated by an awareness of the low intrinsic information rate of speech, a central theme of much of digital speech processing is to obtain a digital representation with lower data rate than that of the sampled waveform.

One of the features which has bothered researchers in the area of speech synthesis in the past has been voicing. We discuss this here because it is a good example of how failure to understand the differences between abstract and physical modeling can lead to disproportionate problems (Keating 1984). The difficulty has arisen because of the nonlinearity of the correlation between the cognitive phonological voicing and how the feature is rendered phonetically. Phonological voicing is a distinctive feature in that, it is a parameter of phonological segments the presence or absence of which is able to change one underlying segment into another. For example, the English alveolar stop /d/ is [+voice] (has voicing) and differs on this feature from the alveolar stop / t / which is [-voice] (does not have voicing). Like all phonological different features, the representation is binary, meaning in this case that [voice] is either present or absent in any one segment.

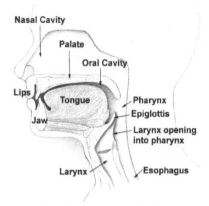

Fig. 2. Anatomy of vocal fold

The most frequent phonetic parameter to correlate with phonological voicing is vocal cord vibration. The vocal cords usually vibrate when the underlying plan is to produce a [+voice] sound, but usually do not when the underlying plan is to produce a [-voice] sound.

Many synthesis models assume constant voicing vocal-cord vibration, but it is quite clear that the binary distinction of vocal-cord vibration vs. no vocal-cord vibration is not accurate. Vocal-cord vibration can begin abruptly (as when there is a glottal stop onset to make this possible singers regularly do this), gradually (the usual case), or at some point during the phone, although it may be phonologically voiced. Similarly for phonologically voiceless segments, it is certainly not the case that on every occasion there is no vocal-cord vibration present at some point during the phone. We know of no model which sets out the conditions under which these variants occur.

Phonological characterizations of segments should not be considered as though they were phonetic, and sets of acoustical features should not be given one-to-one correlation with phonological features. More often than not the correlation is not linear nor, apparently, consistent- though it may yet turn out to be consistent in some respects. Phonology and phonetics cannot be linked simply by using phonological terms within the phonetic domain such as the common transfer of the term voicing between the two levels. Abstract voicing is very different from physical voicing, which is why we consistently use different terms for the two. The basis of the terminology is different for the two levels; and it is bad science to equate the two so directly.

Major problem in speech processing is to represent the shape and characteristics of the vocal tracts. This task is normally done by using an acoustics tube model, based on the calculation of the area function. A Mathematical model of Vocal fold has been obtained as part of new approach for Noise cancellation.

2. The physics of sound production

Speech is the unique signal generated by the human vocal apparatus. Air from the lungs is forced through the vocal tract, generating acoustic waves that are radiated from the lips as a

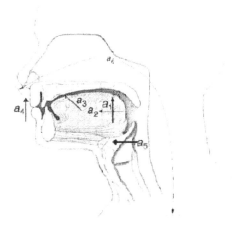

Fig. 3. Articulatory model

pressure field. The physics of this process is well understood, giving us important insights into (sound) speech communication.

The rudiments of speech generation are given in next two sections. Thorough treatments of this important subject can be found in [Flanagan] and [Rabiner and Schafer].

2.1 Development of speech

An young child for the first few months of his life goes on hearing the words being spoken by the persons around him, suppose he has heard the word 'AMMA' serval times spoken by his parents etc., Then he goes on thinking about the production of that word with his audio psychic area ties to reproduce with different movements of his lips, tongue etc., This will be effected by his audio-motor area thus after a few trials the child will be able to reproduce that word. the speech is nothing but a modified expiratory act produced while the expiratory air vibrates the vocal cords of the larynx, and altered by the movements of different structures like tongue, lips, etc.

2.2 The human vocal apparatus

Fig:2 shows a representation of the mid sagittal section of the human vocal tract [Coker]. In this model, the cross-sectional area of the oral cavity $A(x)$, from the glottis, $x = 0$, to the lips, $x = L$, is determined by five parameters: a_1, tongue body height; a_2, anterior/posterior position of the tongue body; a_3, tongue tip height; a_4, mouth opening; and a_5, pharyngeal opening. In addition, a sixth parameter, a_6, is used to additively alter the nominal 17-cm vocal tract length. The articulatory vector a is $(a_1, a_2, ..., a_6)$.

The vocal tract model has three components: an oral cavity, a glottal source, and an acoustic impedance at the lips. We shall consider them singly first and then in combination. As is commonly done, we assume that the behavior of the oral cavity is that of a lossless acoustic

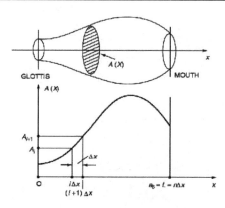

Fig. 4. The acoustic tube model of the vocal tract and its area function

tube of slowly varying in time and space cross-sectional area, A(x), in which plane waves propagate in one dimension (see Fig:3). [Sondhi] and [Portnoff] have shown that under these assumptions, the pressure, p(x, t), and volume velocity, u(x, t), satisfy

The vocal tract model has three components: an oral cavity, a glottal source, and an acoustic impedance at the lips. We shall consider them singly first and then in combination. As is commonly done, we assume that the behavior of the oral cavity is that of a lossless acoustic tube of slowly varying (in time and space) cross-sectional area, A(x), in which plane waves propagate in one dimension. [Sondhi] and [Portnoff] have shown that under these assumptions, the pressure, p(x, t), and volume velocity, u(x, t), satisfy

$$-\frac{\partial p}{\partial x} = \frac{\rho}{A(x,t)}\frac{\partial u}{\partial t} \tag{1}$$

and

$$-\frac{\partial u}{\partial x} = \frac{A(x,t)}{\rho c^2}\frac{\partial p}{\partial t} \tag{2}$$

which express Newton's law and conservation of mass, respectively. In above stated equation ρ is the equilibrium density of the air in the tube and c is the corresponding velocity of sound. Differentiating (eq:1) and (eq:2) with respect to time and space, respectively, and then eliminating the mixed partials, we get the well-known Webster equation [Webster] for pressure,

$$\frac{\partial^2 p}{\partial x^2} + \frac{1}{A(x,t)}\frac{\partial p \partial A}{\partial x \partial x} = \frac{1}{c^2}\frac{\partial^2 p}{\partial t^2} \tag{3}$$

The eigenvalues of (eq:3) are taken as formant frequencies. It is preferable to use the Webster equation (in volume velocity) to compute a sinusoidal steady-state transfer function for the acoustic tube including the effects of thermal, viscous, and wall losses.

To do so we let $p(x,t) = P(x,\omega)$ and $u(x,t) = U(x,\omega)$, where ω is angular frequency. When p and u have this form, (eq:1) and (eq:2) become (cf. [Rabiner, L.R.and Schafer, R.W.]) and

$$p(x,t) = P(x,\omega) \tag{4}$$

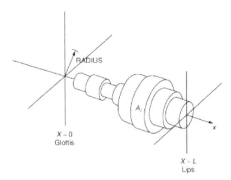

Fig. 5. The discretized acoustic tube model of the vocal tract

$$u(x,t) = U(x,\omega) \tag{5}$$

respectively. In order to account for the losses we define $Z(x,\omega)$ and $Y(x,\omega)$ to be the generalized acoustic impedance and admittance per unit length, respectively. Differentiating (eq:5) with respect to x and substituting for $\frac{-dp}{dx}$ and P from (eq:4) and (eq:5), respectively, we obtain

$$\frac{d^2U}{dx^2} = \frac{1}{Y(x,\omega)} \frac{dU}{dx} \frac{dY}{dx} - Y(x,\omega)Z(x,\omega)U(x,\omega) \tag{6}$$

This is recognized as the *"lossy"* Webster equation for volume velocity. The sinusoidal steady-state transfer function of the vocal tract can be computed by discretizing (eq:6) in space and obtaining approximate solutions to the resulting difference equation for a sequence of frequencies. Let us write U_i^k to signify $U(i\Delta x, k\Delta \omega)$ where the spatial discretization assumes $\Delta x = \frac{L}{n}$ with i = 0 at the glottis and i = n at the lips, as is shown in Fig:4. Similarly, we choose $\Delta \omega = \frac{\Omega}{N}$ and let $0 \le k \le N$. We shall define A_i, Y_i^k, and Z_i^k in an analogous manner. Approximating second derivatives by second central differences and first derivatives by first backward differences, the finite difference representation of (eq:6) is given by (eq:7)

$$U_{i+1}^k = U_i^k \left(3 + (\Delta x)^2 Z_i^k Y_i^k - \frac{Y_{i-1}^k}{Y_i^k} \right) + U_{i-1}^k \left(\frac{Y_{i-1}^k}{Y_i^k} - 2 \right) \tag{7}$$

Given suitable values for U_0^k and U_1^k for $0 \le k \le N$, we can obtain the desired transfer functions from (eq:7). We must find appropriate expressions for Y and Z to account for the losses. Losses arise from thermal effects and viscosity and primarily due to wall vibrations. A detailed treatment of the wall losses is found in [Portnoff] and is summarized by [Rabiner and Schafer]. Portnoff assumes that the walls are displaced $\xi(x,t)$ in a direction normal to the flow due to the pressure at x only. The vocal tract walls are modeled by a damped spring-mass system for which the relationship between pressure and displacement is

$$p(x,y) = M\frac{\partial^2 \xi}{\partial t^2} + b\frac{\partial \xi}{\partial t} + k(x)\xi(x,t) \tag{8}$$

where M, b, and k(x) are the unit length wall mass, damping coefficient, and spring constant, respectively. The displacement of the walls is assumed to perturb the area function about a neutral position according to

$$A(x,t) = A(x) + S(x)\xi(x,t) \tag{9}$$

where A(x) and S(x) are the neutral area and circumference, respectively. By substituting (eq:1) into (eq:2), ignoring higher-order terms, transforming into the frequency domain, Portnoff goes on to observe that the effect of vibrating walls is to add a term to the acoustic admittance in (eq:5), where

$$Y_w(x,t) = j\omega S(x,\omega) \left(\frac{[k(x) - \omega^2 M] - j\omega b}{[k(x) - \omega^2 M]^2 + \omega^2 b^2} \right) \tag{10}$$

The other losses that we wish to consider are those arising from viscous friction and thermal conduction. The former can be accounted for by adding a real quantity Z_v to the acoustic impedance in (eq:4),

$$Z_v(x,\omega) = \frac{S(x)}{A^2(x)} \left(\frac{\omega\rho\mu}{2} \right)^{\frac{1}{2}} \tag{11}$$

Here μ is the viscosity of air. The thermal losses have an effect which is described by adding a real quantity Y_T to the acoustic admittance in (eq:5), where

$$Y_T(x,\omega) = \frac{S(x)(\eta - 1)}{\rho c^2} \left(\frac{\lambda\omega}{2C_p\rho} \right)^{\frac{1}{2}} \tag{12}$$

Here A is the coefficient of heat conduction, η is the adiabatic constant, and C_p is the heat capacity. All the constants are, of course, for air at the conditions of temperature, pressure, and humidity found in the vocal tract. In view of (eq:1), (eq:2), (eq:10), (eq:11) and (eq:12) it is possible to set

$$Z(x,\omega) = \frac{j\omega\rho}{A(x) + Z_v(x,\omega)} \tag{13}$$

and

$$Y(x,\omega) = \frac{j\omega A(x)}{\rho c^2} + Y_w(x,\omega) + Y_T(x,\omega) \tag{14}$$

There are two disadvantages to this approach. First, (eq:13) and (eq:14) are computationally expensive to evaluate. Second, (eq:10) requires values for some physical constants (saliva, phlegm, tonsils, etc.,) of the tissue forming the vocal tract walls. Estimates of these constants are available in [Rabiner, L.R.and Schafer, R.W.] and [Webster]. A computationally simpler empirical model of the losses which agrees with the measurements has been proposed by [Sondhi] in which

$$Z(x,\omega) = \frac{j\omega\rho}{A(x)} \tag{15}$$

and

$$Y(x,\omega) = \frac{A(x)}{\rho c^2} \left(j\omega + \frac{\omega_0^2}{\alpha + j\omega} + (\beta j\omega) \right)^{\frac{1}{2}} \tag{16}$$

Sondhi [10] has chosen values for the constants, $w_0 = 406\pi$, $\alpha = 130\pi$, $\beta = 4$, which he then shows give good agreement with measured formant bandwidths. Moreover, the form of the model agrees with the results of Portnoff, which becomes clear when we observe that $Y_w(x,\omega)$ in (eq:10) will have the same form as the second term on the right-hand side of (eq:16) if

$k(x)\equiv0$ and the ratio of circumference to area is constant. In fact, Portnoff used $k(x) = 0$ and this assumption is reasonable. The third term in the right-hand side of (eq:16) is of the same form as (eq:11) and (eq:12) (under the assumption that the ratio of S to A is constant) by noting that

$$(j\omega)^{\frac{1}{2}} = (1+j)\left(\left(\frac{\omega}{2}\right)\right)^{\frac{1}{2}} \tag{17}$$

2.3 Boundary conditions

With a description of the vocal tract in hand, we can turn our attention to the boundary conditions. Following [Flanagan], the glottal excitation has been assumed to be a constant volume source with an asymmetric triangular waveform of amplitude V . [Dunn et al.] have analyzed such a source in detail. What is relevant is that the spectral envelope decreases as the square of frequency. We have therefore taken the glottal source $U_g(\omega)$ to be

$$U_g(\omega) = \frac{V}{\omega^2} \tag{18}$$

For the boundary condition at the mouth, the well-known [Portnoff] and [Rabiner and Schafer] relationship between sinusoidal steady-state pressure and volume velocity, is used.

$$P(L,\omega) = Z_r(\omega)U(L,\omega) \tag{19}$$

Here the radiation impedance Z_r is taken as that of a piston in an infinite plane baffle, the behavior of which is well approximated by

$$Z_r(\omega) = \frac{j\omega L_r}{\left(\frac{1+j\omega L_r}{R}\right)} \tag{20}$$

Values of the constants which are appropriate for the vocal tract model are given by [Flanagan] as

$$R = \frac{128}{9\pi^2} \tag{21}$$

and

$$L_r = 8\left[A(L)/\pi\right]^{\frac{1}{2}} /3\pi c \tag{22}$$

It is convenient to solve (eq:6) with its boundary conditions (eq:19) and (eq:20) by solving a related initial-value problem for the transfer function

$$H(\omega) = U(L,\omega)/U(0,\omega) \tag{23}$$

$$-\frac{dU}{dx}|_{x=L} = \frac{A(L)}{\rho c^2}(j\omega)P(L,\omega) \tag{24}$$

From which the frequency domain difference equation is

$$-\frac{U_n^k - U_{n-1}^k}{\Delta x} = jk\Delta\omega\frac{A_n}{\rho c^2}P_n^k \tag{25}$$

been derived. Let it be noted from (eq:21), finally, the vocal track output is obtained by (eq:26)

$$\xi(x,t) = e^{1/2 \frac{\left(-b+\sqrt{b^2-4k(x)M}\right)t}{M}} + e^{-1/2 \frac{\left(b+\sqrt{b^2-4k(x)M}\right)t}{M}} - \frac{1}{\sqrt{b^2-4k(x)M}}$$

$$- \left(\int p(x,t) e^{1/2 \frac{\left(b+\sqrt{b^2-4k(x)M}\right)t}{M}} dt\right) e^{-1/2 \frac{\left(b+\sqrt{b^2-4k(x)M}\right)t}{M}}$$

$$+ \left(\int p(x,t) e^{-1/2 \frac{\left(-b+\sqrt{b^2-4k(x)M}\right)t}{M}} dt\right) e^{1/2 \frac{\left(-b+\sqrt{b^2-4k(x)M}\right)t}{M}} \left(e^{-\frac{bt}{M}}\right) \tag{26}$$

Here, p represents pressure, $k(x)$ - Damping coefficient, M - Mass of speech, $\xi(x,t)$ - resultant Value. [NRR]

3. Non- stationary speech signal

The speech signal is the solution to equation(eq:3) Since the function A(x,t) is continuously varyinging time,the solution, p(t),is a non-stationary random change in time. Fortunately, A(x,t) is slowly time-varying with respect to p(t).That is,

$$\overline{P}_k = \overline{P}(k\Delta\omega) = H(k\Delta\omega)U_g(k\Delta\omega)Z_r(k\Delta\omega) \tag{27}$$

$$\left|\frac{\partial A}{\partial t}\right| << \left|\frac{\partial p}{\partial t}\right| \tag{28}$$

Equation (eq:28) may be taken to mean that p(t) is quasi-stationary or piecewise stationary. As such, p(t) can be considered to be a sequence of intervals within each one of which p(t) is stationary. It is true that there are rapid articulatory gestures that violate (eq:28), but in general the quasi-stationary assumption is useful.

4. Fluid dynamical effects

Equation (eq:3) predicts the formation of planar acoustic waves as a result of air flowing into the vocal tract according to the boundary condition of (xyz). However, the Webster equation ignores any effects that the convective air flow may have on the function p(t).

If, instead of (eq:1) and (eq:2), we consider two-dimensional wave propagation, conservation of mass can be written as

$$\frac{\partial u}{\partial x} = \frac{\partial u}{\partial y} = -M^2 \frac{\partial p}{\partial t} \tag{29}$$

where M is the Mach number.
We can also include the viscous and convective effects by observing

$$\frac{\partial u_x}{\partial t} = -\frac{\partial p}{\partial x} - \frac{\partial(u_x u_y)}{\partial x} + \frac{\partial}{\partial x}\left[\frac{1}{N_R}\left(\frac{\partial u_x}{\partial x} + \frac{\partial u_y}{\partial x}\right) - \overline{\mu_x \mu_y}\right] \tag{30}$$

$$\frac{\partial u_y}{\partial t} = -\frac{\partial p}{\partial y} - \frac{\partial(u_x u_y)}{\partial y} + \frac{\partial}{\partial y}\left[\frac{1}{N_R}\left(\frac{\partial u_x}{\partial y} + \frac{\partial u_y}{\partial y}\right) - \overline{\mu_x \mu_y}\right] \tag{31}$$

In (eq:30) and (eq:31) the first term on the right-hand side is recognized as Newton's law expressed in (eq:1) and (eq:2). The second term represents the convective flow. The third term accounts for viscous shear and drag at Reynolds number, NR, and the last term represents turbulence.

Equations (eq:29),(eq:30) and (eq:31) are known as the normalized, two-dimensional, Reynolds averaged, Navier - Stokes equations for slightly compressible flow. These equations can be solved numerically for p(t). The solutions are slightly different from those obtained from (eq:3) due to the formation of vortices and transfer of energy between the convective and wave propagation components of the fluid flow. Typical solutions for the articulatory configuration of Fig: 2 are shown in eqns. (eq:5) and (eq:6). There is reason to believe that (eq:29),(eq:30) and (eq:31) provide a more faithful model of the acoustics of the vocal apparatus than the Webster equation does [11].

5. Noise cancellation

The conclusion to be drawn from the previous two sections is that information is encoded in the speech signal in its short-duration amplitude spectrum [Rabiner, L.R. and Schafer, R.W.]. This implies that by estimating the power spectrum of the speech signal as a function of time, we can identify the corresponding sequence of sounds. Because the speech signal x(t) is non-stationary it has a time-varying spectrum that can be obtained from the time-varying Fourier transform, $X_n(\omega)$. Note that x(t) is the voltage analog of the sound pressure wave, p(t), obtained by solving (eq:3).

5.1 Algorithm

1. Read b, t, M, k(x)
2. $d = b^2 - 4 * k(x) * M$
3. $z = \sqrt{d}$
4. $u = -b + z$
5. $v = b + z$
6. Get the value of f→ function
7. Read lower and upper limits
8. Read n→ numbr of iterations
9. $h = \frac{(upper - lower)}{2}$
10. $S = F(a)$
11. for i = 1: 2: (n-1) (odd)
12. x = a+$h.*i$
13. S = S+4$* f(x)$
14. end
15. for i=2:2:(n-2)
16. x = a + $h.*i$

17. $S = S + 2 * f(x)$

18. end

19. $S = S + f(b)$

20. $A = h * \frac{S}{3}$

21. Repeat the step 6 to 20

22. $B = h * \frac{S}{3}$

23. Obtained values are substuited $\xi(x,t) = exp(0.5 * u * t/M) + exp(-0.5 * v * t/M) + \frac{1}{z} * [A * exp(t * z/M) - B * exp(-0.5 * v * t/M)]$

24. Plot the sequence in the polar graph

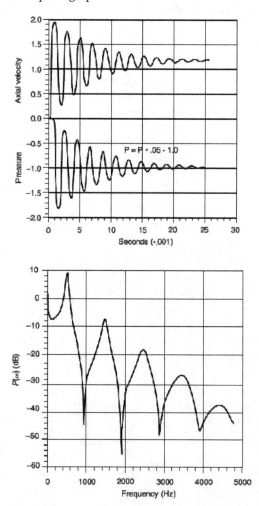

Fig. 6. Speech signals and their spectrum obtained by solving the *NavierStokes* equations

The result is obtained by implementation of the equation (eq:26) in MATLAB. The various values for the pressure, Damping co-efficient and mass is considered for the implementation of the noise cancellation. The graphs are plotted with basic, mid and high damping efficiency (Fig: 7, Fig: 8 and Fig: 9) respectively. Fig: 10 shows the original signal with noise and without noise through the equation (eq:26). From this it can be concluded that the equation can be implemented for active noise cancellation.

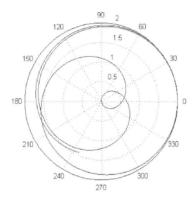

Fig. 7. The acoustic tube model of the vocal tract with basic damping efficiency

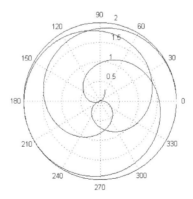

Fig. 8. The acoustic tube model of the vocal tract with Mid damping efficiency

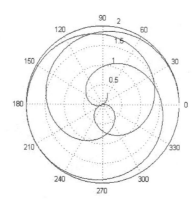

Fig. 9. The acoustic tube model of the vocal tract with high damping efficiency

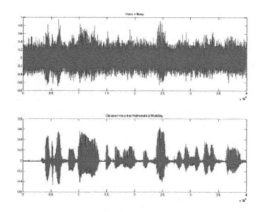

Fig. 10. (a) voice + Noise (b) Voice obtained through modeling

6. Conclusion

Producing an opposing signal (anti-noise) with the same amplitude as the noise you want to reduce (unwanted noise) but with the opposite phase, yields a significant reduction in the noise level. ANC tries to eliminate sound components by adding the exact opposite sound. The level of attenuation is highly dependent on the accuracy of the system for producing the amplitude and the phase of the reductive signal (anti-noise).

The mathematical modeling of vocal fold will recognize only the voice it never create a signal opposite to the noise. It will feed only the vocal output and not the noise, Since it uses shape and characteristic of speech.

The parameters of clean speech sample considered for testing of the algorithms were: duration 2 seconds, PCM 22.050 kHz, 8 bit mono sample recorded under laboratory conditions. This

	Female	Male
Fundamental frequency F_0 (Hz)	207	119
Glottal peak flow	0.14	0.23
Closed quotient	0.26	0.39

Table 1. Properties of the glottal wave (Normal phonation)

Configuration	Thickness lip	Length lip
Basic	0.25	7
Long lip	0.25	9
Short lip	0.25	5
Higher opening	0.25	7
Trapered	0.25(bottom) 0.125 (free tip)	7
thin lip	0.125	7

Table 2. Properties of Mouth

Background noise	Parametric background quality
High	Hissing - Fizzing
Mid	Rushing - Roaring
Low	Rumbling -Rolling
Buzz	Humming - Buzzing
Flutter	Bubbling - Percolating
Static	Crackling - Staticky

Table 3. Parametric estimationof noise

Noise	MMVF	LMS	RLS	AFA	NLMS
acoustic	28.341	23.988	18.729	22.669	20.146
Short	23.105	19.769	20.161	18.083	20.019
White	30.142	20.581	25.105	28.565	26.206
Echo and fading	26.231	21.499	19.281	20.042	26.165

Table 4. Result Obtained

speech signal is used as a benchmark for speech processing. Various noises were generated and added to the original speech signal. The SNR of the signal corrupted with the noise was 8 dB. A linear combination of the generated noise and the original signal is used as the primary input. The outputs SNR of the denoised speech signal are calculated.

MMVF - Mathematical modeling of Vocal fold
LMS - Least mean square
RLS - Recursive least square
AFA - Adaptive filter algorithm (Adaptive RLS)
NLMS - Normalized LMS

7. References

[1] N. R. Raajan, Y. Venkaaramani, & T. R. Sivaramakrishnan *A novel approach to noise cancellation for communication devices*, Instrumentation Science and Technology, Taylor and Francis group, Volume 37, Issue 6, PP: 720-729, 2009.

[2] Fitch, H. L. *Reclaiming temporal information after dynamic time warping.*, J. Acoust. Soc. Amer. 1983 , 74 (Suppl. 1), 816.

[3] Coker, C. H. *A model of articulatory dynamics and control*, Proc. IEEE, pp. 452-460, 1989.

[4] Portnoff, M. R. *A quasi-one-dimensional digital simulation for the time varying vocal tract.*,Masters thesis, MIT, 1973.

[5] Rabiner, L. R. & Schafer, R. W. *Digital Processing of Speech Signals*, Prentice Hall: Englewood Cliffs, NJ, 1978.

[6] Sondhi, M. M. *Model for wave propagation in a lossy vocal tract.*, PP. 1070 - 1075, J. Acoust. Soc. Amer. 1974, PP:55 - 67.

[7] Webster, A. G. *Acoustical impedance and the theory of horns.*, Proc. Nat. Acad. Sci. 1919, PP. 275-282.

Voice Conversion

Jani Nurminen[1], Hanna Silén[2], Victor Popa[2],
Elina Helander[2] and Moncef Gabbouj[2]
[1]*Accenture*
[2]*Tampere University of Technology*
Finland

1. Introduction

Voice conversion (VC) is an area of speech processing that deals with the conversion of the perceived speaker identity. In other words, the speech signal uttered by a first speaker, the *source* speaker, is modified to sound as if it was spoken by a second speaker, referred to as the *target* speaker. The most obvious use case for voice conversion is *text-to-speech* (TTS) synthesis where VC techniques can be used for creating new and personalized voices in a cost-efficient manner. Other potential applications include security related usage (e.g. hiding the identity of the speaker), vocal pathology, voice restoration, as well as games and other entertainment applications. Yet other possible applications could be speech-to-speech translation and dubbing of television programs.

Despite the increased research attention that the topic has attracted, voice conversion has remained a challenging area. One of the challenges is that the perception of the quality and the successfulness of the identity conversion are largely subjective. Furthermore, there is no unique correct conversion result: when a speaker utters a given sentence multiple times, each repetition is different. Due to these reasons, time-consuming listening tests must be used in the development and evaluation of voice conversion systems. The use of listening tests can be complemented with some objective quality measures approximating the subjective rating, such as the one proposed in (Möller, 2000).

Before diving deeper into different aspects of voice conversion, it is essential to understand the factors that determine the perceived speaker identity. Speech conveys a variety of information that can be categorized, for example, into linguistic and nonlinguistic information. Linguistic information has not traditionally been considered in the existing VC systems but is of high interest for example in the field of speech recognition. Even though some hints of speaker identity exist on the linguistic level, nonlinguistic information is more clearly linked to speaker individuality. The nonlinguistic factors affecting speaker individuality can be linked into sociological and physiological dimensions that both have their effect on the acoustic speech signal. Sociological factors, such as the social class, the region of birth or residence, and the age of the speaker, mostly affect the speaking style that is acoustically realized predominantly in prosodic features, such as pitch contour, duration of words, rhythm, etc. The physical attributes of the speaker (e.g. the anatomy of the vocal tract), on the other hand, strongly affect the spectral content and determine the individual voice quality. Perceptually, the most important acoustic features characterizing speaker individuality include the third and the fourth formant, the fundamental frequency and the closing phase of the glottal wave, but the specific parameter importance varies from speaker to speaker and from listener to listener (Lavner et al., 2001).

The vast majority of the existing voice conversion systems deal with the conversion of spectral features, and that will also be the main focus of this chapter. However, prosodic features, such as F_0 movements and speaking rhythm, also contain important cues of identity: in (Helander & Nurminen, 2007b) it was shown that pure prosody alone can be used, to an extent, to recognize speakers that are familiar to us. Nevertheless, it is usually assumed that relatively good results can be obtained through a simple statistical mean and variance scaling of F_0 conversion methods, sometimes together with average speaking rate modification. More advanced prosody conversion techniques have also been proposed for example in (Chapell & Hansen, 1998; Gillet & King, 2003; Helander & Nurminen, 2007a).

A typical voice conversion system is depicted in Figure 1. To convert the source features into target features, a training phase is required. During training, a conversion model is generated to capture the relationship between the source and target speech features, after which the system is able to transform new, previously unseen utterances of the source speaker. Consequently, training data from both the source and the target speaker is usually required. Typical sizes of training sets are usually rather small. Depending on the targeted use case, the data used for the training can be either parallel, i.e. the speakers have uttered the same sentences, or non-parallel. The former is also sometimes referred to as text-dependent and the latter text-independent voice conversion. The most extreme case of text-independent voice conversion is cross-lingual conversion where the source and the target speakers speak different languages that may have different phoneme sets.

In practice, the performance of a voice conversion system is rather dependent on the particular speaker pair. In the most common problem formulation illustrated in Figure 1, it is assumed that we only have data from one source and one target speaker. However, there are voice conversion approaches that can utilize speech from more than two speakers. In *hidden Markov model* (HMM) based speech synthesis, an average voice model trained from multi-speaker data can be adapted using speech data from the target speaker as shown in Figure 2. Furthermore, the use of eigenvoices (Toda et al., 2007a) is another example of an approach utilizing speech from many speakers. In the eigenvoice method, originally developed for speaker adaptation (Kuhn et al., 2000), the parameters of any speaker are formed as a linear combination of eigenvoices. Yet another unconventional approach is to build a model of only the target speaker characteristics without having the source speaker data available in the training phase (Desai et al., 2010).

Numerous different VC approaches have been proposed in the literature. One way to categorize the VC techniques is to divide them into methods used for stand-alone voice conversion and the adaptation techniques used in HMM-based speech synthesis. The former methods are discussed in Section 2 while Section 3 focuses on the latter. Speech parameterization and modification issues that are relevant for both scenarios are introduced in the next subsection. Finally, at the end of the chapter, we will provide a short discussion on the remaining challenges and possible future directions in voice conversion research.

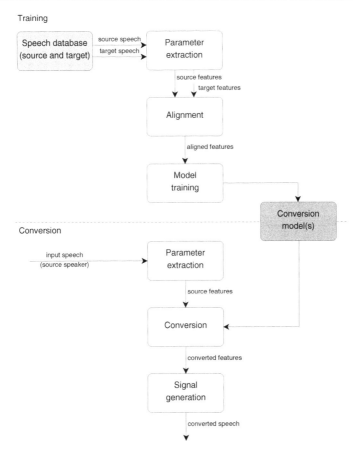

Fig. 1. Block diagram illustrating stand-alone voice conversion. The training phase generates conversion models based on training data that in the most common scenario includes speech from both source and target speakers. In the conversion phase, the trained models can be used for converting unseen utterances of source speech.

1.1 Speech parameterization and modification

Most of the voice conversion approaches use segmental feature extraction to find a set of representative features that are then converted from source to target speakers. In principle, the features to be transformed in voice conversion can be any parameters describing the speaker-dependent factors of speech. The parameterization of the speech and the flexibility of the analysis/synthesis framework have a fundamental effect on the quality of converted speech. Hence, the parameterization should allow easy modification of the perceptually important characteristics of speech as well as to provide high-quality waveform resynthesis.

The most popular speech representations are based on the source-filter model. In the source-filter model, the glottal airflow is represented as an excitation signal that can be thought to take the form of a pulse train for the voiced sounds and the form of a noise signal for the unvoiced sounds. A voiced excitation is characterized by a fundamental frequency or

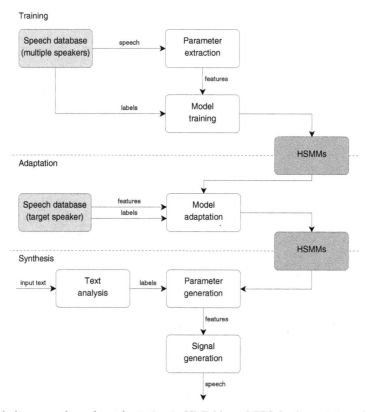

Fig. 2. Block diagram of speaker adaptation in HMM-based TTS. In the training phase, HSMMs are generated using speech data from multiple speakers. Then, model adaptation is applied to obtain HSMMs for a given target speaker. The adapted HSMMs can be used in TTS synthesis for producing speech with the target voice.

pitch that is determined by the oscillation frequency of the vocal folds. The vocal tract is seen as a resonator cavity that shapes the excitation signal in frequency, and can be understood as a filter having its resonances at formant frequencies. The use of formants as VC features would in theory be a highly attractive alternative that has been studied in (Narendranath et al., 1995; Rentzos et al., 2004) but the inherent difficulties in reliable estimation and modification of formants have prevented wider adoption, and the representations obtained by simple mathematical methods have remained the preferred solution.

The use of linear prediction, and in particular the line spectral frequency (LSF) representation has been highly popular in VC research (Arslan, 1999; Erro et al., 2010a; Nurminen et al., 2006; Tao et al., 2010; Turk & Arslan, 2006), due to its favorable interpolation properties and the close relationship to the formant structure. In addition to the linear prediction based methods, cepstrum-based parameterization has been widely used, for example in the form of Mel-frequency cepstrum coefficients (MFCCs) (Stylianou et al., 1998).

Standard linear prediction coefficients give information on the formants (peaks) but not the valleys (spectral zeros) in the spectrum whereas cepstral processing treats both peaks and valleys equally. The generalized Mel-cepstral analysis method (Tokuda et al., 1994) provides a unification that offers flexibility to balance between them. The procedure is controlled by two parameters, α and γ, where γ balances between the cepstral and linear prediction representations and α describes the frequency resolution of the spectrum. Mel-cepstral coefficients (MCCs) ($\gamma = 0$, $\alpha = 0.42$ for 16 kHz speech) are a widely used representation in both VC and HMM-based speech synthesis (Desai et al., 2010; Helander et al., 2010a; Toda et al., 2007b; Tokuda et al., 2002).

The modification techniques based on the source-filter model use different ways to estimate and convert the excitation and vocal tract filter parameters. In mixed mode excitation (Fujimura, 1968), the level of devoicing is included typically as bandwise mean aperiodicity (BAP) of some frequency sub-bands, and the excitation signal is reconstructed as a weighted sum of voiced and unvoiced signals. An attractive alternative is to use the sinusoidal model developed by McAulay and Quatieri (McAulay & Quatieri, 1986) in which the speech or the excitation is represented as a sum of time-varying sinusoids whose amplitude, frequency and phase parameters are estimated from the short-time Fourier transform using a peak-picking algorithm. This framework lends itself to time and pitch scale modifications producing high-quality results. A variant of this approach has been successfully used in (Nurminen et al., 2006).

STRAIGHT vocoder (Kawahara et al., 1999) is a widely used analysis/synthesis framework for both stand-alone voice conversion and HMM-based speech synthesis. It decomposes speech into a spectral envelope without periodic interferences, F_0, and relative voice aperiodicity. The STRAIGHT-based speech parameters are further encoded, typically into MCCs or LSFs, logarithmic F_0, and bandwise mean aperiodicities. Alternative speech parameterization schemes include harmonic plus stochastic model (Erro et al., 2010a), glottal modeling using inverse filtering (Raitio et al., 2010), and frequency-domain two-band voicing modeling (Kim et al., 2006; Silén et al., 2009). It is also possible to operate directly on spectral domain samples (Sündermann & Ney, 2003).

Table 1 provides a summary of typical features used in voice conversion. It should be noted that any given voice conversion system utilizes only a subset of the features listed in the table. Some voice conversion systems may also operate on some other features, not listed in Table 1.

2. Stand-alone voice conversion

The first step in the training of a stand-alone voice conversion system is data alignment. To be able to model the differences between the source and target speakers, the relationship needs to be captured using similar data from both speakers. While it is intuitively clear that proper alignment is needed for building high-quality models, the study presented in (Helander et al., 2008) demonstrated that simple frame-level alignment using *dynamic time warping* (DTW) offers sufficient accuracy when the training data is parallel. More detailed discussion, especially covering more difficult use cases, is considered to be outside the scope of this chapter but it should be noted that relevant studies have been published in the literature: for example, text-independent voice conversion is discussed in (Tao et al., 2010) and cross-lingual conversion in (Sündermann et al., 2006). In the strict sense, the alignment step may also be omitted through model adaptation techniques which can, for instance, adapt an already trained conversion model.

Feature	Notes
LSFs	Offer stability, good interpolation properties, and close relationship to formants. Model spectral peaks.
MFCCs	Model both spectral peaks and valleys. Reliable for measuring acoustic distances and thus useful especially for alignment.
MCCs	Perhaps the most widely used features for representing spectra both in stand-alone conversion and in HMM based synthesis. Benefits e.g. in alignment very similar to those of MFCCs.
Formants	Formant bandwidths, locations and intensities would be highly useful features in VC but reliable estimation is extremely challenging.
Spectral samples	Spectral domain samples can also be used as VC features. Typically used in warping based conversion.
F_0	F_0 or log F_0 are typically mean-shifted and scaled to the values of the target speaker.
Voicing	At least binary voicing or aperiodicity information is typically used. More refined voicing information may also be employed.
Excitation spectra	Sometimes details of the excitation spectra need to be modeled as well, for example when using sinusoidal modeling.

Table 1. Examples of speech features commonly used in voice conversion.

2.1 Basic approaches

The most popular voice conversion approach in the literature has been *Gaussian mixture model* (GMM) based conversion (Kain & Macon, 1998; Stylianou et al., 1998). The data is modeled using a GMM and converted by a function that is a weighted sum of local regression functions. A GMM can be trained to model the density of source features only (Stylianou et al., 1998) or the joint density of both source and target features (Kain & Macon, 1998). Here we review the approach based on a joint density GMM (Kain & Macon, 1998).

First, let us assume that we have aligned source and target vectors $\mathbf{z} = [\mathbf{x}^T, \mathbf{y}^T]^T$ that can be used to train a conversion model. Here, $\mathbf{x}$ and $\mathbf{y}$ correspond to the source and target feature vectors, respectively. In the training, the aligned data $\mathbf{z}$ is used to estimate the GMM parameters (α, μ, Σ) of the joint distribution $p(\mathbf{x}, \mathbf{y})$ (Kain & Macon, 1998). This is accomplished iteratively through the well-known Expectation Maximization (EM) algorithm (Dempster et al., 1977).

The conditional probability of the converted vector $\mathbf{y}$ given the input vector $\mathbf{x}$ and the mth Gaussian component is a Gaussian distribution characterized by mean $\mathbf{E}_m^{(y)}$ and the covariance

$\mathbf{D}_m^{(y)}$:

$$\mathbf{E}_m^{(y)} = \boldsymbol{\mu}_m^{(y)} + \boldsymbol{\Sigma}_m^{(yx)}\left(\boldsymbol{\Sigma}_m^{(xx)}\right)^{-1}\left(\mathbf{x} - \boldsymbol{\mu}_m^{(x)}\right)$$

$$\mathbf{D}_m^{(y)} = \boldsymbol{\Sigma}_m^{(yy)} - \boldsymbol{\Sigma}_m^{(yx)}\left(\boldsymbol{\Sigma}_m^{(xx)}\right)^{-1}\boldsymbol{\Sigma}_m^{(xy)} \tag{1}$$

and the minimum mean square error (MMSE) solution for the converted target $\hat{\mathbf{y}}$ is:

$$\hat{\mathbf{y}} = \sum_{m=1}^{M} \omega_m \mathbf{E}_m^{(y)} = \sum_{m=1}^{M} \omega_m \left[\boldsymbol{\mu}_m^{(y)} + \boldsymbol{\Sigma}_m^{(yx)}\left(\boldsymbol{\Sigma}_m^{(xx)}\right)^{-1}\left(\mathbf{x} - \boldsymbol{\mu}_m^{(x)}\right)\right]. \tag{2}$$

Here ω_m denotes the posterior probability of the observation $\mathbf{x}$ for the mth Gaussian component:

$$\omega_m = \frac{\alpha_m \mathcal{N}\left(\mathbf{x}; \boldsymbol{\mu}_m^{(x)}, \boldsymbol{\Sigma}_m^{(xx)}\right)}{\sum_{j=1}^{M} \alpha_j \mathcal{N}\left(\mathbf{x}; \boldsymbol{\mu}_j^{(x)}, \boldsymbol{\Sigma}_j^{(xx)}\right)}, \tag{3}$$

and the mean $\boldsymbol{\mu}_m$ and covariance $\boldsymbol{\Sigma}_m$ of the mth Gaussian distribution are defined as:

$$\boldsymbol{\mu}_m = \begin{bmatrix} \boldsymbol{\mu}_m^{(x)} \\ \boldsymbol{\mu}_m^{(y)} \end{bmatrix}, \quad \boldsymbol{\Sigma}_m = \begin{bmatrix} \boldsymbol{\Sigma}_m^{(xx)} & \boldsymbol{\Sigma}_m^{(xy)} \\ \boldsymbol{\Sigma}_m^{(yx)} & \boldsymbol{\Sigma}_m^{(yy)} \end{bmatrix}. \tag{4}$$

The use of GMMs in voice conversion has been extremely popular. In the next subsection, we will discuss some shortcomings of this method and possible solutions for overcoming the main weaknesses.

Another basic voice conversion technique is codebook mapping (Abe et al., 1988). The simplest way to realize codebook based mapping would be to train a codebook of combined feature vectors $\mathbf{z}$. Then, during conversion, the source side of the vectors could be used for finding the closest codebook entry, and the target side of the selected entry could be used as the converted vector. The classical paper on codebook based conversion (Abe et al., 1988) proposes a slightly different approach that can utilize existing vector quantizers. There the training phase involves generating histograms of the vector correspondences between the quantized and aligned source and target vectors. These histograms are then used as weighting functions for generating a linear combination based mapping codebook. Regardless of the details of the implementation, codebook based mapping offers a very simple and straightforward approach that can capture the speaker identity quite well, but the result suffers from frame-to-frame discontinuities and poor prediction capability on new data. Some enhancements to the basic codebook based methods are presented in Section 2.3.

Finally, we consider frequency warping to offer the third very basic approach for voice conversion. In this method, a warping function is established between the source and target spectra. In the simplest case, the warping function can be formed based on spectra representing a single voiced frame (Shuang et al., 2006). Then, during the actual conversion, the frequency warping function is directly applied to the spectral envelope. The frequency warping methods can at best obtain very high speech quality but have limitations regarding the success of identity conversion, due to problems in preserving the shape of modified spectral peaks and controlling the bandwidths of close formants. Proper controlling of the formant amplitudes is also challenging. Furthermore, the use of only a single warping function can be considered a weakness. To overcome this, proposals have been made to utilize several warping functions (Erro et al., 2010b) but the above-mentioned fundamental problems remain largely unsolved.

2.2 Problems and improvements in GMM-based conversion

GMM-based voice conversion has been a dominating technique in VC despite its problems. In this section, we review some of the problems and solutions proposed to overcome them.

The control of model complexity is a crucial issue when learning a model from data. There is a trade-off between two objectives: model fidelity and the generalization-capability of the model for unseen data. This trade-off problem, also referred to as bias-variance dilemma (Geman et al., 1992), is common for all model fitting tasks. In essence, simple models are subject to oversmoothing, whereas the use of complex models may result in overfitting and thus in poor prediction ability on new data. In addition to oversmoothing and overfitting, a major problem in conventional GMM-based conversion, as well as in many codebook based algorithms, is the time-independent mapping of features that ignores the inherent temporal correlation of speech features.

2.2.1 Overfitting

In GMM-based VC, overfitting can be caused by two factors: first, the GMM may be overfitted to the training set as demonstrated in Figure 3. Second, when a mapping function is estimated, it may also become overfitted.

In particular, a GMM with full covariance matrices is difficult to estimate and is subject to overfitting (Mesbashi et al., 2007). With unconstrained (full) covariance matrices, the number of free parameters grows quadratically with the input dimensionality. Considering for example 24-dimensional source and target feature vectors and a joint-density GMM model with 16 mixture components and full covariance matrices, 18816 $(((2\text{x}24)\text{x}(2\text{x}24)/2+24)\text{x}16)$ variance terms are to be estimated. One solution is to use diagonal covariance matrices $\Sigma^{xx}, \Sigma^{xy}, \Sigma^{yx}, \Sigma^{yy}$ with an increased number of components. In the joint-density GMM, this results in converting each feature dimension separately. In reality, however, the pth spectral descriptor of the source may not be directly related to the pth spectral descriptor of the target, making this approach inaccurate.

Overfitting of the mapping function can be avoided by applying partial least squares (PLS) for regression estimation (Helander et al., 2010a); a source GMM (usually with diagonal covariance matrices) is trained and a mapping function is then estimated using partial least squares regression between source features weighted by posterior probability for each Gaussian and the original target features.

2.2.2 Oversmoothing

Oversmoothing occurs both in frequency and in the time domain. In frequency domain, this results in losing fine details of the spectrum and in broadening of the formants. In speech coding, it is common to use post-filtering to emphasize the formants (Kondoz, 2004) and similarly post-filtering can also be used to improve the quality of the speech in voice conversion. It has also been found that combining the frequency warped source spectrum

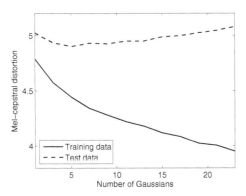

Fig. 3. Example of overfitting. Increasing the number of Gaussians reduces the distortion for the training data but not necessarily for a separate test set because the model might be overfitted to the training set.

with the GMM-based converted spectrum reduces the effect of oversmoothing by retaining more spectral details (Toda et al., 2001)

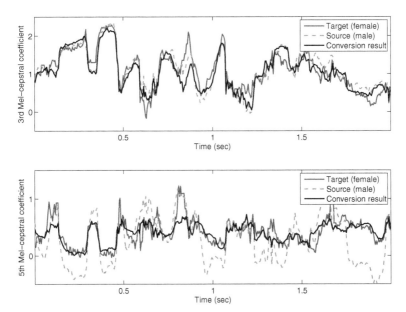

Fig. 4. Example of oversmoothing. Linear transformation of spectral features is not able to retain all the details and causes oversmoothing. The conversion result (black line) is achieved using linear multivariate regression to convert the source speaker's MCCs (dashed gray line) to match with the target speaker's MCCs (solid gray line).

In time domain, the converted feature trajectory has much less variation than the original target feature trajectory. This phenomenon is illustrated in Figure 4. According to (Chen et al.,

2003), oversmoothing occurs because the term $\Sigma_m^{yx}(\Sigma_m^{xx})^{-1}$ (Equation 1) becomes close to zero and thus the converted target becomes only a weighted sum of means of GMM components as

$$\hat{\mathbf{y}} = \sum_{m=1}^{M} \omega_m \boldsymbol{\mu}_m^{(y)}. \tag{5}$$

To avoid the problem, the source GMM can be built from a larger data set and only the means are adapted using maximum a posteriori estimation (Chen et al., 2003). Thus, the converted target becomes:

$$\hat{\mathbf{y}} = \mathbf{x} + \sum_{m=1}^{M} \omega_m \left(\boldsymbol{\mu}_m^{(y)} - \boldsymbol{\mu}_m^{(x)} \right). \tag{6}$$

Global variance can be used to compensate for the reduced variance of the converted speech feature sequence with feature trajectory estimation (Toda et al., 2007b). Alternatively, the global variance can be accounted already in the estimation of the conversion function; this degrades the objective performance but improves the subjective quality (Benisty & Malah, 2011).

2.2.3 Time-independent mapping

The conventional GMM-based method converts each frame regardless of other frames and thus ignores the temporal correlation between consecutive frames. This can lead to discontinuities in feature trajectories and thus degrade perceptual speech quality. It has been shown that there is usually only a single mixture component that dominates in each frame in GMM-based VC approaches (Helander et al., 2010a). This makes the conventional GMM-based approaches to shift from a soft acoustic classification method to a hard classification method, making it susceptible to discontinuities similarly as in the case of codebook based methods.

Solving the time-independency problem of GMM-based conversion was proposed in (Toda et al., 2007b) through the introduction of maximum likelihood (ML) estimation of the spectral parameter trajectory. Static source and target feature vectors are extended with first-order deltas, i.e $\mathbf{z} = [\mathbf{x}^T, \Delta\mathbf{x}^T, \mathbf{y}^T, \Delta\mathbf{y}^T]^T$ and a joint-density GMM is estimated. In synthesis, both converted mean and covariance matrices (Equation 1) are used to generate the target trajectory. The trajectory estimation is similar to HMM-based speech synthesis described in Section 3.1.1. A recent approach (Helander et al., 2010b) bears some similarity to (Toda et al., 2007b) by using the relationship between the static and dynamic features to obtain the optimal speech sequence but does not use the transformed mean and (co)variance from the GMM-based conversion. To obtain smooth feature trajectory, the converted features can be low-pass filtered after conducting the GMM-based transformation (Chen et al., 2003) or the GMM posterior probabilities can be smoothed before making the conversion (Helander et al., 2010a). Instead of frame-wise transformation of the source spectral features, in (Nguyen & Akagi, 2008) each phoneme was modeled to consist of event targets and these event targets were used as conversion features.

2.3 Advanced codebook-based methods

The basic codebook mapping (Abe et al., 1988) introduced in Section 2.1 is affected by several important limitations. A fundamental problem of codebook mapping is the discrete representation of the acoustic spaces as a limited set of spectral envelopes. Another severe problem is caused by the frame-based operation which ignores the relationships between neighboring frames or any information related to the temporal evolution of the parameters. These problems produce spectral discontinuities and lead to a degraded quality of the converted speech. In terms of spectral mapping, though, the codebook has the attractive property of preserving the details that appear in the training data.

The above issues have been addressed in a number of articles and several have been proposed to improve the spectral continuity of the codebook mapping. A selection of methods will be presented in this section, including weighted linear combination of codewords (Arslan, 1999), hierarchical codebook mapping (Wang et al., 2005), local linear transformation (Popa et al., 2012) and trellis structured vector quantization (Eslami et al., 2011). It is worth mentioning that these algorithms have their own limitations.

2.3.1 Weighted linear combination of codewords

Weighted linear combination of codewords (Arslan, 1999) addresses the problem of discrete representation of the acoustic space by utilizing a weighted sum of codewords in order to cover well the acoustic space of the target speaker. Phoneme centroids are computed for both the source and the target speaker, forming two codebooks of spectral vectors with one-to-one correspondence.

In order to convert a source vector, a set of weights is determined depending on a similarity measure between the source vector and the set of centroids in the source codebook. The conversion is realized by using the weights to linearly combine the corresponding centroids in the target codebook. While improving the continuity with respect to the basic codebook approach, this method causes severe oversmoothing by summing over a wide range of different spectral envelopes.

2.3.2 Hierarchical codebook mapping

Hierarchical codebook mapping (Wang et al., 2005) aims to improve the precision of the spectral conversion by estimating and adding a residual term to the typical codeword mapping. In addition to the mapping codebook between the source vectors $\mathbf{x}$ and the target vectors $\mathbf{y}$, a new codebook is trained from the same source vectors $\mathbf{x}$ and the corresponding conversion residuals $\epsilon = \mathbf{y} - \hat{\mathbf{y}}$. The residuals represent the differences between a real target vector $\mathbf{y}$ aligned to $\mathbf{x}$ and $\mathbf{x}$'s conversion through the first codebook, $\hat{\mathbf{y}}$. In conversion, both codebooks are used; the first for predicting a target codeword $\hat{\mathbf{y}}$ and the second to find the corresponding residual ϵ. The final result of the conversion is obtained by summing outputs of the two codebooks, i.e. $\hat{\mathbf{y}}' = \hat{\mathbf{y}} + \epsilon$. Although hierarchical codebook mapping improves to some extent the precision compared to the basic codebook based conversion, this approach is essentially only producing a finer representation of the acoustic space while being otherwise likely to inherit the fundamental problems of the basic codebook mapping.

2.3.3 Local linear transformation

Methods based on linear transformations such as GMM typically compute a number of linear transformations corresponding to different acoustic classes and use a linear combination of these transformations to convert a given spectral vector. As discussed in Section 2.2.2, this effectively causes the problem of oversmoothing characterized by smoothed spectra and parameter tracks. The local linear transformation approach reduces the oversmoothing by operating with neighboring acoustic vectors that share similar properties (Popa et al., 2012). Linear regression models are estimated from neighborhoods of source-target codeword pairs with similar acoustic properties. Each spectral vector is converted with an individual linear transformation determined in the least squares sense from a subset of nearby codewords.

In order to convert a source spectral vector $\mathbf{x}$, the first step is to select a set of nearest codewords in the source speaker's codebook. Assuming a one-to-one mapping between the codebooks of the source and target speakers, we can estimate in the second step, in the least squares sense, a linear transformation β_0 between the selected source and target codewords. The result of the linear transformation $\mathbf{y}_0^T = \mathbf{x}^T \beta_0$ is used next to refine the selection of source-target codeword pairs by replacing the old set with the joint codewords nearest to $\left[\mathbf{x}^T, \mathbf{y}_0^T\right]^T$. A new linear transformation β_1 is estimated from the newly selected neighborhood leading to an updated conversion result $\mathbf{y}_1^T = \mathbf{x}^T \beta_1$. The iteration of the last neighborhood selection and the linear transformation estimation steps was found to be pseudo-convergent. It was also found beneficial to estimate band diagonal matrices β_i instead of full ones. An entire sequence of spectral vectors is converted by repeating the above procedure for each vector.

The main idea of this method is in line with (Wang et al., 2004) that proposed a phoneme-tied weighting scheme which splits the codebook into groups by phoneme types. At the same time, the discontinuities typical to the basic codebook mapping are alleviated due to the overlapping of neighborhoods from consecutive frames. The conversion-time computation is somewhat intensive and can be regarded as a drawback.

2.3.4 Trellis structured vector quantization

Trellis structured vector quantization (Eslami et al., 2011) tackles the problem of discontinuities common for many codebook-based conversion approaches. The method operates with blocks of consecutive frames to obtain dynamic information and uses a trellis structure and dynamic programming to optimize a codeword path based on this dynamic information.

Parallel training speech quantized in the form of codeword sequences is aligned and source-target codeword pairs are formed. Preceding codewords in the source and target sequences are combined with each pair forming blocks of consecutive codewords which reflect the speech dynamics. The conversion of a source speech sequence requires the construction of an equally long trellis structure whose lines correspond to the codewords of the target codebook. The nodes in the trellis structure are assigned an initial cost and a maximum number of so-called survivor paths, or valid preceding target codewords. The initial cost is based on the similarities between the consecutive frames from the input sequence and memorized blocks of consecutive source codewords while the survivor paths are selected based on memorized blocks of consecutive target codewords. The survivor paths are also associated a transition cost based on Euclidean distance. Dynamic programming is used to find the optimal path in the trellis structure resulting in a converted sequence of target codewords.

The method proposes a rigorous way to handle the spectral continuity by utilizing dynamic information and keeping at the same time the advantages of good preservation of spectral details provided by the codebook framework. The approach was shown to clearly outperform the basic GMM and codebook-based techniques which are known to suffer from oversmoothing and discontinuities respectively.

2.4 Bilinear models

The bilinear approach reformulates the spectral envelope representation from e.g. line spectral frequencies to a two-factor parameterization corresponding to speaker identity and phonetic information. The spectral vector y^{sc}, uttered by speaker s and corresponding to the phonetic content class c, is represented as a product of a speaker-dependent matrix A^s and a phonetic content vector b^c using the asymmetric bilinear model (Popa et al., 2011):

$$y^{sc} = A^s b^c. \tag{7}$$

If the training set contains an equal number of spectral vectors for each speaker and in each content class, a closed form procedure exists for fitting the asymmetric model using *singular value decomposition* (SVD) (Tenenbaum & Freeman, 2000).

As discussed in the introduction, the usual problem formulation of voice conversion can be extended by considering the case of generating speech with a target voice, using parallel speech data from multiple source speakers. The alignment of the training data (S source speakers and one target speaker) is a prerequisite step for model estimation and is usually handled using DTW. On the other hand, the alignment of the test data (S utterances of the source speakers) is also required if $S > 1$.

A so-called *complete* data is formed by concatenating the aligned training and test data of the S source speakers. Considering each aligned S-tuple a separate class of phonetic content, an asymmetric bilinear model is fit to the *complete* data following the closed-form SVD procedure described in (Tenenbaum & Freeman, 2000). With the *complete* data arranged as a stacked matrix Y:

$$Y = \begin{bmatrix} y^{11} & \cdots & y^{1C} \\ \cdots & \cdots & \cdots \\ y^{S1} & \cdots & y^{SC} \end{bmatrix}, \tag{8}$$

where C denotes the total number of aligned frames in the *complete* data, the equations of the asymmetric bilinear model can be rewritten as:

$$Y = AB, \tag{9}$$

where $A = \begin{bmatrix} A^1 \\ \cdots \\ A^S \end{bmatrix}$ and $B = \begin{bmatrix} b^1 & \cdots & b^C \end{bmatrix}$. The SVD of the *complete* data $Y = UZV^T$ is used

to determine the parameters A as the first J columns of UZ and B as first J rows of V^T where J is the model dimensionality chosen according to some precision criterion and where the diagonal elements of Z are considered to be in decreasing eigenvalue order. This yields a matrix A^s for each source speaker s and a vector b^c for each phonetic content class c in the *complete* data (hence producing also the b^cs of the test utterance).

The model adaptation to the target voice t can be done in closed form using the phonetic content vectors b^c learned during training. Suppose the aligned training data from our target speaker t consists of M spectral vectors which by convention we considered to be in M different phonetic content classes $\mathbf{C}_T = \{c_1, c_2, \ldots, c_M\}$. We can derive the speaker-dependent matrix $\mathbf{A}^t$ that minimizes the total squared error over the target training data

$$E^* = \sum_{c \in \mathbf{C}_T} \left\| \mathbf{y}^{tc} - \mathbf{A}^t \mathbf{b}^c \right\|^2. \tag{10}$$

The missing spectral vectors in the target voice t and a phonetic content class c of the test sentence can be then synthesized from $\mathbf{y}^{tc} = \mathbf{A}^t \mathbf{b}^c$. This means we can estimate the target version of the test sentence by multiplying the target speaker matrix $\mathbf{A}^t$ with the phonetic content vectors corresponding to the test sentence.

The performance of the bilinear approach was found close to that of a GMM-based conversion with optimal number of Gaussian components particularly for reduced training sets. The method benefits of efficient computational algorithms based on SVD. On the downside, the bilinear approach suffers from oversmoothing problem, similarly as many other VC techniques (e.g. GMM-based conversion).

2.5 Nonlinear methods

Artificial neural networks offer a powerful tool for modeling complex (nonlinear) relationships between input and output. They have been applied to voice conversion for example in (Desai et al., 2010). The main disadvantage is the requirement of massive tuning when selecting the best architecture for the network. Another alternative to model nonlinear relationships is kernel partial least squares regression (Helander et al., 2011); a kernel transformation is carried out on the source data as a preprocessing step and PLS regression is applied on kernel transformed data. In addition, the kernel transformed source data of the current frame is augmented from kernel transformed source data from the previous and next frames before regression calculation. This helps in improving the accuracy of the model and maintaining the temporal continuity that is a major problem of many voice conversion algorithms. In (Song et al., 2011), support vector regression was used for non-linear spectral conversion. Compared to neural networks, the tuning of support vector regression is less demanding.

3. Voice transformation in text-to-speech synthesis

Text-to-speech or speech synthesis refers to artificial conversion of text into speech. Currently the most widely studied TTS methods are corpus-based: they rely on the use of real recorded speech data. The quality of a text-to-speech system can be measured in terms of how well the synthesized speech can be understood, how natural-sounding it is, and how well the synthesis captures the speaker identity of the training speech data.

Statistical parametric speech synthesis, such as *hidden Markov model* (HMM) based speech synthesis (Tokuda et al., 2002; Yoshimura et al., 1999), provides a flexible framework for TTS with good capabilities for speaker or style adaptation. In this kind of synthesis, the recorded speech data is parameterized into a form that enables control of the perceptually important features of speech, such as the spectrum and the fundamental frequency. Statistical modeling is then used to create models for the speech features based on the labeled training data. The training procedure is quite similar to training in HMM-based speech recognition, but now all of the speech features needed for the analysis/synthesis framework are modeled. The parameters of synthetic speech are generated from the state output and duration statistics of the context-dependent HMMs corresponding to a given input label sequence. Waveform resynthesis is used for creating the actual synthetic speech signal.

In HMM-based speech synthesis, even a relatively small database can be used to produce understandable speech. Models can be easily adapted, and producing new voices or altering speech characteristics such as emotions is easy. The statistical models of an existing HMM voice, trained using data either from one speaker (a speaker-dependent system) or multiple speakers (a speaker-independent system) are adapted using a small amount of data from the target speaker. A typical approach employs linear regression to map the models for the target speaker. The mapping functions are typically different for different sets of models allowing the individual conversion functions to be simple. This is in contrast to for example the GMM-based voice conversion discussed in Section 2.1 that attempts to provide a global conversion model consisting of several linear transforms. In stand-alone VC, it is common to rely on acoustic information only, but in TTS, the phonetic information is usually readily available and can be effectively utilized.

In the following, we discuss the transformation techniques applied in HMM-based speech synthesis. We first give an overview on the basic HMM modeling techniques required both in speaker-dependent and speaker-adaptive synthesis. After that we discuss the speaker adaptive synthesis where the average models are transformed using a smaller set of data from a specific target speaker. For the most of the discussed ideas, the implementations are publicly available in Hidden Markov Model-Based Speech Synthesis System (HTS) (Tokuda et al., 2011). HTS is a widely used and extensive framework for HMM-based speech synthesis containing tools for both HMM-based speech modeling and parameter generation as well as for speaker adaptation.

3.1 Statistical modeling of speech features for synthesis

Speech modeling using context-dependent HMMs, common for both speaker-dependent and speaker-adaptive synthesis, are described in the following. Many of the core techniques originate from HMM-based speech recognition summarized in (Rabiner, 1989).

3.1.1 HMM modeling of speech

HMM-based speech synthesis provides a flexible framework for speech synthesis, where all speech features can be modeled simultaneously within the same multi-stream HMM. Spectral parameter modeling involves continuous-density HMMs with single multivariate Gaussian distributions and typically diagonal covariance matrices or mixtures of such Gaussian distributions. In F_0 modeling, multi-space probability distribution HMMs (MSD-HMM) with two types of distributions are used: continuous densities for voiced speech segments and a single symbol for unvoiced segments. A typical modeling scheme uses 5-state left-to-right modeling with no state skipping. In addition to the state output probability distributions the modeling also involves the estimation of state transition probabilities indicating the probability of staying in the state or transferring to the next one.

The training phase aims at determining model parameters of the HMMs based on the training data. These parameters include means and covariances of the state output probability distributions and probabilities of the state transitions. This parameter set λ^* that maximizes the likelihood of the training data $\mathbf{O}$ is:

$$\lambda^* = \arg\max_{\lambda} P(\mathbf{O}|\lambda) = \arg\max_{\lambda} \sum_{all\ \mathbf{q}} P(\mathbf{O}, \mathbf{q}|\lambda). \tag{11}$$

Here $\mathbf{q}$ is a hidden variable denoting an HMM state sequence, each state having output probability distributions for each speech feature and transition probability. Due to the hidden variable there is no analytical solution for the problem. A local optimum can be found using Baum-Welch estimation.

The use of acceptable state durations is essential for high-quality synthesis. Hence, in addition to the speech features such as spectral parameters and F_0, a model for the speech rhythm is needed as well. It is modeled through the state duration distributions employing either Gaussian (Yoshimura et al., 1998) or Gamma distributions and in the synthesis phase these state duration distributions are used to determine how many frames are generated from each HMM state. In the conventional approach, the duration distributions are derived from the statistics of the last iteration of the HMM training. The duration densities are used in synthesis but they are not present in the standard HMM training. A more accurate modeling can be achieved using hidden semi-Markov model (HSMM) based techniques (Zen et al., 2004) where the duration distributions are explicitly present already during the parameter re-estimation of the training phase.

In the synthesis phase, the trained HMMs are used to generate speech parameters for text unseen in the training data. Waveform resynthesis then turns these parameters into an acoustic speech waveform using e.g. vocoding. A sentence HMM is formed by concatenating the required context-dependent state models. The maximum likelihood estimate for the synthetic speech parameter sequence $\mathbf{O} = \{\mathbf{o}_1, \mathbf{o}_2, \dots, \mathbf{o}_T\}$ is (Tokuda et al., 2000):

$$\mathbf{O}^* = \arg\max_{\mathbf{O}} P(\mathbf{O}|\lambda, T). \tag{12}$$

The solution of Equation 12 can be approximated by dividing the estimation into the separate search of the optimal state sequence $\mathbf{q}^*$ and maximum likelihood observations $\mathbf{O}^*$ given the state sequence:

$$\mathbf{q}^* = \arg\max_{\mathbf{q}} P(\mathbf{q}|\lambda, T)$$
$$\mathbf{O}^* = \arg\max_{\mathbf{O}} P(\mathbf{O}|\mathbf{q}^*, \lambda, T). \tag{13}$$

To introduce continuity in synthesis, dynamic modeling is typically used. Without the delta-augmentation the parameter generation algorithm would only output a sequence of mean vectors corresponding to the state sequence $\mathbf{q}^*$. The delta-augmented observation vectors $\mathbf{o}_t$ contain both static $\mathbf{c}_t$ and dynamic feature values $\Delta\mathbf{c}_t$:

$$\mathbf{o}_t = \left[\mathbf{c}_t^T, \Delta\mathbf{c}_t^T\right]^T, \tag{14}$$

where the dynamic feature vectors $\Delta\mathbf{c}_t$ are defined as:

$$\Delta\mathbf{c}_t = \mathbf{c}_t - \mathbf{c}_{t-1}. \tag{15}$$

This can be written in the matrix form as $\mathbf{O} = \mathbf{WC}$:

$$\underbrace{\begin{bmatrix} \vdots \\ \mathbf{c}_{t-1} \\ \Delta\mathbf{c}_{t-1} \\ \mathbf{c}_t \\ \Delta\mathbf{c}_t \\ \mathbf{c}_{t+1} \\ \Delta\mathbf{c}_{t+1} \\ \vdots \end{bmatrix}}_{\mathbf{O}} = \underbrace{\begin{bmatrix} \cdots & \vdots & \vdots & \vdots & \vdots & \cdots \\ \cdots & 0 & \mathbf{I} & 0 & 0 & \cdots \\ \cdots & -\mathbf{I} & \mathbf{I} & 0 & 0 & \cdots \\ \cdots & 0 & 0 & \mathbf{I} & 0 & \cdots \\ \cdots & 0 & -\mathbf{I} & \mathbf{I} & 0 & \cdots \\ \cdots & 0 & 0 & 0 & \mathbf{I} & \cdots \\ \cdots & 0 & 0 & -\mathbf{I} & \mathbf{I} & \cdots \\ \cdots & \vdots & \vdots & \vdots & \vdots & \cdots \end{bmatrix}}_{\mathbf{W}} \underbrace{\begin{bmatrix} \vdots \\ \mathbf{c}_{t-2} \\ \mathbf{c}_{t-1} \\ \mathbf{c}_t \\ \mathbf{c}_{t+1} \\ \vdots \end{bmatrix}}_{\mathbf{C}} \tag{16}$$

If the state output probability distributions are modeled as single Gaussian distributions, the ML solution for a feature sequence $\mathbf{C}^*$ is:

$$\mathbf{C}^* = \arg\max_{\mathbf{C}} P(\mathbf{WC}|\mathbf{q}^*, \lambda, T) = \arg\max_{\mathbf{C}} \mathcal{N}(\mathbf{WC}; \boldsymbol{\mu}_{\mathbf{q}^*}, \boldsymbol{\Sigma}_{\mathbf{q}^*}), \tag{17}$$

where $\boldsymbol{\mu}_{\mathbf{q}^*}$ and $\boldsymbol{\Sigma}_{\mathbf{q}^*}$ refer to the mean and covariance of the state output probabilities of the state sequence $\mathbf{q}^*$. The solution of Equation 17 can be found in a closed form.

HMM-based speech synthesis suffers from the same problem as GMM-based voice conversion: the statistical modeling loses fine details and introduces oversmoothing in the generated speech parameter trajectories. Postfiltering of the generated spectral parameters can be utilized to improve the synthesis quality. Another widely used approach for restoring the natural variance of the speech parameters is to use global variance modeling (Toda & Tokuda, 2007) in speech parameter generation.

3.1.2 Labeling with rich context features

The prosody of HMM-based speech synthesis is controlled by the context-dependent labeling. It tries to capture the language-dependent contextual variation in the speech unit waveforms. Separate models are trained for each phoneme in different contexts. In addition to phoneme identities, a large set of other phonetic and prosodic features related to for instance position, stress, accent, part of speech and number of different phonetic units are used to make a distinction between different context-dependent phonemes. No high-level linguistic knowledge is needed and instead, the characteristics of the speech in different contexts are automatically learned from the training data. In (Tokuda et al., 2011), the following features are included in context-dependent labeling of English data:

Phoneme level: Phoneme identity of the current and two preceding/succeeding phonemes and position in a syllable.

Syllable level: Number of phonemes/accent/stress of the current/preceding/ succeeding syllable, position in a word/phrase, number of preceding/succeeding stressed/accented syllables in a phrase, distance from the previous/following stressed/accented syllable, and phoneme identity of the syllable vowel.

Word level: Part of speech of the current/preceding/succeeding word, number of syllables in the current/preceding/succeeding word, position in the phrase, number of preceding/succeeding content words, number of words from previous/next content word.

Phrase level: Number of syllables in the preceding/current/succeeding phrase, position in a major phrase, and ToBI endtone.

Utterance level: Number of syllables/words/phrases in the utterance.

Even though context-dependent labeling enables the separation of different contexts in the modeling, it also makes the training data very sparse. Collecting a training database that would include enough training data to estimate reliable models for all possible context-dependent labels of a language is practically impossible. To pool acoustically similar models and to provide a prediction mechanism for labels not seen in the training data, decision tree clustering using a set of binary questions and the *minimum description length* (MDL) criterion (Shinoda & Watanabe, 2000) is often employed. The construction of a MDL-based decision tree takes into account both the acoustic similarity of the state output probability distributions assigned to each node and the overall complexity of the resulting tree. In the synthesis phase, the input text is parsed to form a context-dependent label sequence and the tree is traversed from the root to the leaves to find the cluster for each synthesis label.

3.2 Changing voice characteristics in HMM-based speech synthesis

Speaker adaptation provides an efficient way of creating new synthetic voices for HMM-based speech synthesis. Once an initial model is trained, either speaker-dependently (SD) or speaker-independently (SI), its parameters can be adapted for an unlimited number of new speakers, speaking styles, or emotions using only a small number of adaptation sentences. An extreme example is given in (Yamagishi et al., 2010), where thousands of new English, Finnish, Spanish, Japanese, and Mandarin synthesis voices were created by adapting the trained average voices using only a limited amount of adaptation sentences from each target speaker.

In adaptive HMM-based speech synthesis, there is no need for parallel data. The adaptation updates the HMM model parameters including the state output probability distributions and the duration densities using data from the target speaker or speaking style. The first speaker adaptation approaches were developed for the standard HMMs but HSMMs with explicit duration modeling have been widely used in adaptation as well. The commonly used methods for speaker adaptation include *maximum a posteriori* (MAP) adaptation (Lee et al., 1991), *maximum likelihood linear regression* (MLLR) adaptation (Leggetter & Woodland, 1995), *structural maximum a posteriori linear regression* (SMAPLR) adaptation (Shiohan et al., 2002), and their variants. In MAP adaptation of HMMs, each Gaussian distribution is updated according to the new data and the prior probability of the model. MLLR and SMAPLR, on the other hand, use linear regression to convert the existing model parameters to match with the characteristics of the adaptation data; to cope with the data sparseness, models are typically clustered and a shared transformation is trained for the models of each cluster. While the MAP-based adaptation can only update distributions that have observations in the adaptation data, MLLR and SMAPLR using linear conversion to transform the existing parameters into new ones are effective in adapting any distributions. The adaptation performance of MLLR or SMAPLR can be further improved by using *speaker-adaptive training* (SAT) to prevent single speaker's data from biasing the training of the average voice.

The above-mentioned HMM adaptation approaches are discussed in more detail in the following. In addition to the MAP and linear regression derivatives originating from the speaker adaptation of HMM-based speech recognition, the adaptation approaches used in stand-alone voice conversion can be applied in HMM-based speech synthesis. In *speaker interpolation* of HMMs (Yoshimura et al., 1997) a set of HMMs from representative speakers is interpolated to form models matching with the characteristics of the target speaker's voice. The interpolation of an HMM set can change the synthetic speech smoothly from the existing voice to the target voice by changing the interpolation ratio. In addition to the speaker adaptation, interpolation can be used for instance in emotion or speaking-style conversion. The *eigenvoice* approach (Shichiri et al., 2002), also familiar from voice conversion (Kuhn et al., 2000), tackles the problem of how to determine the interpolation ratio by constructing a speaker specific super-vector from all the state output mean vectors of each speaker, emotion, or style-dependent HMM set. The dimension of the super-vector is reduced by PCA and the new HMM set is reconstructed from the first eigenvoices (eigenvectors).

3.2.1 Maximum a posteriori adaptation

Maximum a posteriori adaptation of HMMs updates parameters of each state output probability distribution according to the given adaptation data. If we have some knowledge on what the model parameters are likely to be already before observing any data, also a limited amount of data from the target speaker can be enough to adapt the model parameters. In MAP adaptation of HMMs (Lee et al., 1991; Masuko et al., 1997), this prior information of model parameters is taken into account when deriving the new output distributions.

MAP estimate for HMM parameters λ is defined as the mode of the posterior probability distribution $P(\lambda|\mathbf{O})$ given the prior probability $P(\lambda)$ and the data $\mathbf{O} = \{\mathbf{o}_1, \mathbf{o}_2, \ldots, \mathbf{o}_T\}$ (Lee et al., 1991):

$$\bar{\lambda} = \arg\max_{\lambda} P(\lambda|\mathbf{O}) = \arg\max_{\lambda} P(\mathbf{O}|\lambda) P(\lambda). \qquad (18)$$

The speaker-independent models can be used as informative priors that are updated according to the adaptation data. In the MAP adaptation approach of (Masuko et al., 1997), the adaptation data are segmented by Viterbi alignment of HMMs and state means and covariances are updated using the data assigned to the state.

The use of prior information is useful when only a small amount of training data is available. However, every distribution is adapted individually and for a small amount or sparse adaptation data, MAP estimates may be unreliable and there might even be states for which no new set of parameters is trained. This makes the synthesis jump between the average voice and the target voice even within a sentence. Vector-field-smoothing (VFS) (Takahashi & Sagayama, 1995) can be used to alleviate the problem: it uses K nearest neighbor distributions to interpolate means and covariances for the distributions having no adaptation available. A rather similar approach can also be used for smoothing the means and the covariances of the adapted distributions.

3.2.2 Maximum likelihood linear regression adaptation

Adaptation using mapping of the existing HMM distribution parameters according to the adaptation data avoids the MAP adaptation problem of non-updated distributions. HMM adaptation using maximum likelihood linear regression (MLLR) to find such transformations (Leggetter & Woodland, 1995) was first applied in HMM-based speech synthesis in (Tamura et al., 1998). In MLLR adaptation, a linear mapping of the model distributions is found in a way that the likelihood of the adaptation data from the target speaker is maximized. Regression or decision tree-based clustering is used to tie similar models for the adaptation and the transformation is shared across the distributions of each cluster. Sharing the transformations across multiple distributions decreases the amount of data needed for the adaptation. Hence, MLLR-based adaptation often works better than MAP adaptation if only a small amount of data is used (Zen et al., 2009).

The model for the target voice is created by mapping the output probability distributions of an existing voice using a set of linear transforms. The ith multivariate Gaussian distribution of an MLLR-adapted voice is of the form:

$$b_i\left(\mathbf{o}_t\right) = \mathcal{N}\left(\mathbf{o}_t; \zeta\boldsymbol{\mu}_i + \boldsymbol{\epsilon}, \boldsymbol{\Sigma}_i\right) = \mathcal{N}\left(\mathbf{o}_t; \mathbf{W}\boldsymbol{\xi}_i, \boldsymbol{\Sigma}_i\right), \qquad (19)$$

where $\boldsymbol{\mu}_i$ and $\boldsymbol{\Sigma}_i$ are the mean and covariance of the average voice distribution, ζ and $\boldsymbol{\epsilon}$ the mapping and the bias, and $\boldsymbol{\xi}_i = [\boldsymbol{\mu}_i^T, 1]^T$. The transformation $\mathbf{W} = [\zeta, \boldsymbol{\epsilon}]$ is tied across the distributions of each cluster. Transformation $\bar{\mathbf{W}}$ is the one that maximizes the likelihood of the adaptation data $\mathbf{O} = \{\mathbf{o}_1, \mathbf{o}_2, \ldots, \mathbf{o}_T\}$:

$$\bar{\mathbf{W}} = \underset{W}{\arg\max}\, P\left(\mathbf{O}|\lambda, \mathbf{W}\right). \qquad (20)$$

Baum-Welch estimation can be used to find $\bar{\mathbf{W}}$.

In the standard MLLR adaptation, the model means are adapted but the covariances are taken from the existing model. The adaptation of the distribution variances is needed especially in F_0 adaptation. In the constrained MLLR (CMLLR), both the model means and the covariances are transformed using the same set of transformations estimated simultaneously. The adapted means and covariances are transformed from the average voice means and covariances of the existing models using the same transformation matrix ζ:

$$b_i\left(\mathbf{o}_t\right) = \mathcal{N}\left(\mathbf{o}_t; \zeta\boldsymbol{\mu}_i + \boldsymbol{\epsilon}, \zeta\boldsymbol{\Sigma}_i\zeta^T\right). \qquad (21)$$

MLLR-based HMM adaptation of continuous-density spectral parameters can be extended to adapt the parameters of MSD-HMMs of F_0 modeling (Tamura et al., 2001a) and the parameters of the state duration distributions (Tamura et al., 2001b) as well. In HSMM modeling, the state duration distributions are present in the HMM training from the beginning. The transformed HSMM distributions also have the form of Equation 19 or Equation 21 (Yamagishi & Kobayashi, 2007), however, state duration distributions having scalar mean and variance.

3.2.3 Structural maximum a posteriori linear regression adaptation

MLLR and CMMLR adaptation work well in the average voice constructions since there is a lot of training data available from multiple speakers. However, in the model adaptation, the amount of speech data from each target speaker is typically rather small, hence MAP criterion as a more robust one compared to the ML criterion might be more attractive. HMM adaptation by structural maximum a posteriori linear regression (SMAPLR) (Shiohan et al., 2002) combines the idea of linear mapping of the HMM distributions and structural MAP (SMAP) exploiting a tree structure to derive the prior distributions. The use of constrained SMAPLR (CSMAPLR) in adaptive HSMM-based speech synthesis was introduced in (Yamagishi et al., 2009) and it is widely used for the speaker adaptation task in speech synthesis.

Replacing the ML criterion in MLLR with the MAP criterion leads to the model that also takes into account some prior information about the transform $\mathbf{W}$:

$$\bar{\mathbf{W}} = \arg\max_{\mathbf{W}} P\left(\mathbf{W}|\mathbf{O}, \lambda\right) = \arg\max_{\mathbf{W}} P\left(\mathbf{O}|\mathbf{W}, \lambda\right) P\left(\mathbf{W}\right). \tag{22}$$

In the best case, the use of the MAP criterion can help to avoid training of unrealistic transformations that would not generalize that well for unseen content. Furthermore, well selected prior distributions can increase the conversion accuracy. In SMAPLR adaptation (Shiohan et al., 2002), a hierarchical tree structure is used to derive priors that better take into account the relation and similarity of different distributions. For the root node, a global transform is computed using all the adaptation data. Rest of the nodes recursively inherit their prior distributions from their parent nodes: hyperparameters of the parent node posterior distributions $P(\mathbf{W}|\mathbf{O}, \lambda)$ are propagated to the child nodes where the distribution is approximated and used as a prior distribution $P(\mathbf{W})$. In each node the MAPLR transformation $\mathbf{W}$ is derived as in Equation 22 using the prior distribution and the adaptation data assigned to the node.

3.2.4 Speaker adaptive training

The amount of training data from the target speaker is typically small whereas the initial models are usually estimated from a large set of training data preferably spoken by multiple speakers. This *speaker independent* (SI) training with multi-speaker training data resulting in average voice HMM usually provides a more robust basis for the mapping compared to the *speaker-dependent* (SD) training using only single-speaker data (Yamagishi & Kobayashi, 2007). In addition, especially in F_0 modeling larger datasets tend to provide more complete modeling hence making average voice training even more attractive compared to the speaker-dependent modeling (Yamagishi & Kobayashi, 2007).

The average voice used for adaptation should provide high-quality mapping to various target voices and should not have bias from single speakers' data. *Speaker adaptive training* (SAT) of HMMs introduced in (Anastasakos et al., 1996) and applied in HSMM-based speech synthesis in (Yamagishi, 2006; Yamagishi & Kobayashi, 2005), addresses the problem by estimating the average voice parameters simultaneously with the linear-regression-based transformation reducing the influence of speaker differences. While the SI training aims at finding the best set of model parameters, SAT searches for both the speaker adaptation parameters and the average voice parameters that provide the maximum likelihood result in the transformation.

In SAT, the set of HSMM model parameters λ_{SAT} and the adaptation parameters Λ_{SAT} are optimized jointly for all F speakers using maximum likelihood criterion (Yamagishi & Kobayashi, 2005):

$$(\lambda_{SAT}, \Lambda_{SAT}) = \arg\max_{\lambda,\Lambda} P\left(\mathbf{O}|\lambda, \Lambda\right) = \arg\max_{\lambda,\Lambda} \prod_{f=1}^{F} P\left(\mathbf{O}^{(f)}|\lambda, \Lambda^{(f)}\right). \tag{23}$$

This differs from the SI training where only the model parameters are estimated during the average voice building. The maximization can be done with Baum-Welch estimation.

4. Concluding remarks

The research on voice conversion has been fairly active and several important advances have been made on different fronts. In this chapter, we have aimed to provide an overview covering the basics and the most important research directions. Despite the fact that the state-of-the-art VC methods provide fairly successful results, additional research advances are needed to progress further towards providing excellent speech quality and highly successful identity conversion at the same time. Also, the practical limitations in different application scenarios may offer additional challenges to overcome. For example, in many real-world applications, the speech data is noisy, making the training of high-quality conversion models even more difficult.

There is still room for improvement in all sub-areas of voice conversion, both in stand-alone voice conversion and in speaker adaptation in HMM-based speech synthesis. Recently, there has been a trend shift from text-dependent to text-independent use cases. It is likely that the trend will continue and eventually shift towards cross-lingual scenarios required in the attractive application area of speech-to-speech translation. Also, the two sub-areas treated separately in this chapter will be likely to merge at least to some extent, especially when they are needed in hybrid TTS systems (such as (Ling et al., 2007; Silén et al., 2010)) that combine unit selection and HMM-based synthesis.

An interesting and potentially very important future direction of VC research is enhanced parameterization. The current parameterizations often cause problems with synthetic speech quality, both in stand-alone conversion and in HMM-based synthesis, and the currently-used feature sets do not ideally represent the speaker-dependencies. More realistic mimicking of the human speech production could turn out to be crucial. This topic has been touched in (Z-H. Ling et al., 2009), and for example the use of glottal inverse filtering (Raitio et al., 2010) could also provide another initial step to this direction.

5. References

Abe, M., Nakamura, S., Shikano, K. & Kuwabara, H. (1988). Voice conversion through vector quantization, *Proc. of ICASSP*, pp. 655–658.

Anastasakos, T., McDonough, J. & Schwartz, R. (1996). A compact model for speaker-adaptive training, *Proc. of ICSLP*, pp. 1137–1140.

Arslan, L. (1999). Speaker transformation algorithm using segmental codebooks (STASC), *Speech Communication* 28(3): 211–226.

Benisty, H. & Malah, D. (2011). Voice conversion using GMM with enhanced global variance, *Proc. of Interspeech*, pp. 669–672.

Chapell, D. & Hansen, J. (1998). Speaker-specific pitch contour modelling and modification, *Proc. of ICASSP*, Seattle, pp. 885–888.

Chen, Y., Chu, M., Chang, E., Liu, J. & Liu, R. (2003). Voice conversion with smoothed GMM and MAP adaptation, *Proc. of Eurospeech*, pp. 2413–2416.

Dempster, A. P., Laird, N. M. & Rubin, D. B. (1977). Maximum likelihood from incomplete data via the EM algorithm, *Journal of the Royal Statistical Society: Series B (Statistical Methodology)* 39(1): 1–38.

Desai, S., Black, A., Yegnanarayana, B. & Prahallad, K. (2010). Spectral mapping using artificial neural networks for voice conversion, *IEEE Trans. Audio, Speech, Lang. Process.* 18(5): 954–964.

Erro, D., Moreno, A. & Bonafonte, A. (2010a). INCA algorithm for training voice conversion systems from nonparallel corpora, *IEEE Trans. Audio, Speech, Lang. Process.* 18(5): 944–953.

Erro, D., Moreno, A. & Bonafonte, A. (2010b). Voice conversion based on weighted frequency warping, *IEEE Trans. Audio, Speech, Lang. Process.* 18(5): 922–931.

Eslami, M., Sheikhzadeh, H. & Sayadiyan, A. (2011). Quality improvement of voice conversion systems based on trellis structured vector quantization, *Proc. of Interspeech*, pp. 665–668.

Fujimura, O. (1968). An approximation to voice aperiodicity, *IEEE Trans. Audio Electroacoust.* 16(1): 68–72.

Geman, S., Bienenstock, E. & Doursat, R. (1992). Neural networks and the bias/variance dilemma, *Neural Communication* 4(1): 1–58.

Gillet, B. & King, S. (2003). Transforming F0 contours, *Proc. of Eurospeech*, Geneve, pp. 101–104.

Helander, E. & Nurminen, J. (2007a). A novel method for prosody prediction in voice conversion, *Proc. of ICASSP*, pp. 509–512.

Helander, E. & Nurminen, J. (2007b). On the importance of pure prosody in the perception of speaker identity, *Proc. of Interspeech*, pp. 2665–2668.

Helander, E., Schwarz, J., Nurminen, J., Silén, H. & Gabbouj, M. (2008). On the impact of alignment on voice conversion performance, *Proc. of Interspeech*, pp. 1453–1456.

Helander, E., Silén, H., Miguez, J. & Gabbouj, M. (2010b). Maximum a posteriori voice conversion using sequential Monte Carlo methods, *Proc. of Interspeech*, pp. 1716–1719.

Helander, E., Silén, H., Virtanen, T. & Gabbouj, M. (2011). Voice conversion using dynamic kernel partial least squares regression, *IEEE Trans. Audio, Speech, Lang. Process.* To appear in 2011.

Helander, E., Virtanen, T., Nurminen, J. & Gabbouj, M. (2010a). Voice conversion using partial least squares regression, *IEEE Trans. Audio, Speech, Lang. Process.* 18(5): 912–921.

Kain, A. & Macon, M. W. (1998). Spectral voice conversion for text-to-speech synthesis, *Proc. of ICASSP*, Vol. 1, pp. 285–288.

Kawahara, H., Masuda-Katsuse, I. & de Cheveigné, A. (1999). Restructuring speech representations using a pitch-adaptive time-frequency smoothing and an instantaneous-frequency-based F0 extraction: Possible role of a repetitive structure in sounds, *Speech Communication* 27(3-4): 187–207.

Kim, S.-J., Kim, J.-J. & Hahn, M. (2006). HMM-based Korean speech synthesis system for hand-held devices, *IEEE Trans. Consum. Electron.* 52(4): 1384–1390.

Kondoz, A. M. (2004). *Digital speech coding for low bit rate communication systems*, Wiley and Sons, England.

Kuhn, R., Junqua, J.-C., Nguyen, P. & Niedzielski, N. (2000). Rapid speaker adaptation in eigenvoice space, *IEEE Trans. Speech Audio Process.* 8(6): 695–707.

Lavner, Y., Rosenhouse, J. & Gath, I. (2001). The prototype model in speaker identification by human listeners, *International Journal of Speech Technology* 4: 63–74.

Lee, C.-H., Lin, C.-H. & Juang, B.-H. (1991). A study on speaker adaptation of the parameters of continuous density hidden Markov models, *IEEE Trans. Signal Process.* 39(4): 806–814.

Leggetter, C. & Woodland, P. (1995). Maximum likelihood linear regression for speaker adaptation of continuous density hidden Markov models, *Comput. Speech Lang.* 9(2): 171–185.

Ling, Z.-H., Qin, L., Lu, H., Gao, Y., Dai, L.-R., Wang, R.-H., Jiang, Y., Zhao, Z.-W., Yang, J.-H., Chen, J. & Hu, G.-P. (2007). The USTC and iFlytek speech synthesis systems for Blizzard Challenge 2007, *Proc. of Blizzard Challenge Workshop*.

Masuko, T., Tokuda, K., Kobayashi, T. & Imai, S. (1997). Voice characteristics conversion for HMM-based speech synthesis system, *Proc. of ICASSP*, pp. 1611–1614.

McAulay, R. & Quatieri, T. (1986). Speech analysis/synthesis based on a sinusoidal representation, *IEEE Trans. Acoust., Speech, Signal Process.* 34(4): 744–754.

Mesbashi, L., Barreaud, V. & Boeffard, O. (2007). Comparing GMM-based speech transformation systems, *Proc. of Interspeech*, pp. 1989–1456.

Möller, S. (2000). *Assessment and Prediction of Speech Quality in Telecommunications*, Kluwer Academic Publisher.

Narendranath, M., Murthy, H. A., Rajendran, S. & Yegnanarayana, B. (1995). Transformation of formants for voice conversion using artificial neural networks, *Speech Communication* 16(2): 207–216.

Nguyen, B. & Akagi, M. (2008). Phoneme-based spectral voice conversion using temporal decomposition and Gaussian mixture model, *Communications and Electronics, 2008. ICCE 2008. Second International Conference on*, pp. 224–229.

Nurminen, J., Popa, V., Tian, J., Tang, Y. & Kiss, I. (2006). A parametric approach for voice conversion, *Proc. of TC-STAR Workshop on Speech-to-Speech Translation*, pp. 225–229.

Popa, V., Nurminen, J. & Moncef, G. (2011). A study of bilinear models in voice conversion, *Journal of Signal and Information Processing* 2(2): 125–139.

Popa, V., Silen, H., Nurminen, J. & Gabbouj, M. (2012). Local linear transformation for voice conversion, *submitted to ICASSP*.

Rabiner, L. R. (1989). A tutorial on hidden Markov models and selected applications in speech recognition, *Proceedings of the IEEE* 77(2): 257–286.

Raitio, T., Suni, A., Yamagishi, J., Pulakka, H., Nurminen, J., Vainio, M. & Alku, P. (2010). HMM-based speech synthesis utilizing glottal inverse filtering, *IEEE Trans. Audio, Speech, Lang. Process.* 19(1): 153–165.

Rentzos, D., Vaseghi, S., Q., Y. & Ho, C.-H. (2004). Voice conversion through transformation of spectral and intonation features, *Proc. of ICASSP*, pp. 21–24.

Shichiri, K., Sawabe, A., Yoshimura, T., Tokuda, K., Masuko, T., Kobayashi, T. & Kitamura, T. (2002). Eigenvoices for HMM-based speech synthesis, *Proc. of Interspeech*, pp. 1269–1272.

Shinoda, K. & Watanabe, T. (2000). MDL-based context-dependent subword modeling for speech recognition, *Acoustical Science and Technology* 21(2): 79–86.

Shiohan, O., Myrvoll, T. & Lee, C. (2002). Structural maximum a posteriori linear regression for fast HMM adaptation, *Comput. Speech Lang.* 16(3): 5–24.

Shuang, Z., Bakis, R. & Qin, Y. (2006). Voice conversion based on mapping formants, *TC-STAR Workshop on Speech-to-Speech Translation*, pp. 219–223.

Silén, H., Helander, E., Nurminen, J. & Gabbouj, M. (2009). Parameterization of vocal fry in HMM-based speech synthesis, *Proc. of Interspeech*, pp. 1775–1778.

Silén, H., Helander, E., Nurminen, J., Koppinen, K. & Gabbouj, M. (2010). Using robust Viterbi algorithm and HMM-modeling in unit selection TTS to replace units of poor quality, *Proc. of Interspeech*, pp. 166–169.

Sündermann, D., Höge, H., Bonafonte, A., Ney, H. & Hirschberg, J. (2006). Text-independent cross-language voice conversion, *Proc. of Interspeech*, pp. 2262–2265.

Sündermann, D. & Ney, H. (2003). VTLN-based voice conversion, *Proc. of ISSPIT*, pp. 556–559.

Song, P., Bao, Y., Zhao, L. & Zou, C. (2011). Voice conversion using support vector regression, *Electronics Letters* 47(18): 1045–1046.

Stylianou, Y., Cappe, O. & Moulines, E. (1998). Continuous probabilistic transform for voice conversion, *IEEE Trans. Audio, Speech, Lang. Process.* 6(2): 131–142.

Takahashi, J. & Sagayama, S. (1995). Vector-field-smoothed Bayesian learning for incremental speaker adaptation, *Proc. of ICASSP*, pp. 696–699.

Tamura, M., Masuko, T., Tokuda, K. & Kobayashi, T. (1998). Speaker adaptation for HMM-based speech synthesis system using MLLR, *Proc. of the 3th ESCA/COCOSDA Workshop on Speech Synthesis*, pp. 273–276.

Tamura, M., Masuko, T., Tokuda, K. & Kobayashi, T. (2001a). Adaptation of pitch and spectrum for HMM-based speech synthesis using MLLR, *Proc. of ICASSP*, pp. 805–808.

Tamura, M., Masuko, T., Tokuda, K. & Kobayashi, T. (2001b). Text-to-speech synthesis with arbitrary speaker's voice from average voice, *Proc. of Interspeech*, pp. 345–348.

Tao, J., Zhang, M., Nurminen, J., Tian, J. & Wang, X. (2010). Supervisory data alignment for text-independent voice conversion, *IEEE Trans. Audio, Speech, Lang. Process.* 18(5): 932–943.

Tenenbaum, J. B. & Freeman, W. T. (2000). Separating style and content with bilinear models, *Neural Computation* 12(6): 1247–1283.

Toda, T., Black, A. & Tokuda, K. (2007b). Voice conversion based on maximum-likelihood estimation of spectral parameter trajectory, *IEEE Trans. Audio, Speech, Lang. Process.* 15(8): 2222–2235.

Toda, T., Ohtani, Y. & Shikano, K. (2007a). One-to-many and many-to-one voice conversion based on eigenvoices, *Proc. of ICASSP*, pp. 1249–1252.

Toda, T., Saruwatari, H. & Shikano, K. (2001). Voice conversion algorithm based on Gaussian mixture model with dynamic frequency warping of STRAIGHT spectrum, *Proc. of ICASSP*, pp. 841–844.

Toda, T. & Tokuda, K. (2007). A speech parameter generation algorithm considering global variance for HMM-based speech synthesis, *IEICE Trans. Inf. & Syst.* E90-D: 816–824.

Tokuda, K., Kobayashi, T., Masuko, T. & Imai, S. (1994). Mel-generalized cepstral analysis - a unified approach to speech spectral estimation, *Proc. of ICSLP*, pp. 1043–1046.

Tokuda, K., Kobayashi, T., Masuko, T., Kobayashi, T. & Kitamura, T. (2000). Speech parameter generation algorithms for HMM-based speech synthesis, *Proc. of ICASSP*, pp. 1315–1318.

Tokuda, K., Oura, K., Hashimoto, K., Shiota, S., Zen, H., Yamagishi, J., Toda, T., Nose, T., Sako, S. & Black, A. W. (2011). HMM-based speech synthesis system (HTS).
URL: *http://hts.sp.nitech.ac.jp/*

Tokuda, K., Zen, H. & Black, A. (2002). An HMM-based speech synthesis system applied to English, *Proc. of 2002 IEEE Workshop on Speech Synthesis*, pp. 227–230.

Turk, O. & Arslan, L. (2006). Robust processing techniques for voice conversion, *Computer Speech and Language* 4(20): 441–467.

Wang, Z., Wang, R., Shuang, Z. & Ling, Z. (2004). A novel voice conversion system based on codebook mapping with phoneme-tied weighting, *Proc. of Interspeech*, pp. 1197–1200.

Wang, Y.-P., Ling, Z.-H. & Wang, R.-H. (2005). Emotional speech synthesis based on improved codebook mapping voice conversion, *Proc. of ACII*, pp. 374–381.

Yamagishi, J. (2006). *Average-voice-based speech synthesis*, PhD thesis, Tokyo Institute of Technology.

Yamagishi, J. & Kobayashi, T. (2005). Adaptive training for hidden semi-Markov model, *Proc. of ICASSP*, pp. 365–366.

Yamagishi, J. & Kobayashi, T. (2007). Average-voice-based speech synthesis using HSMM-based speaker adaptation and adaptive training, *IEICE Trans. Inf. & Syst.* E90-D(2): 533–543.

Yamagishi, J., Kobayashi, T., Nakano, Y., Ogata, K. & Isogai, J. (2009). Analysis of speaker adaptation algorithms for HMM-based speech synthesis and a constrained SMAPLR adaptation algorithm, *IEEE Trans. Audio, Speech, and Lang. Process.* 17(1): 66–83.

Yamagishi, J., Usabaev, B., King, S., Watts, O., Dines, J., Tian, J., Guan, Y., Hu, R., Oura, K., Wu, Y.-J., Tokuda, K., Karhila, R. & Kurimo, M. (2010). Thousands of voices for HMM-based speech synthesis – Analysis and application of TTS systems built on various ASR corpora, *IEEE Trans. Audio, Speech, and Lang. Process.* 18(5): 984–1004.

Yoshimura, T., Masuko, T., Tokuda, K., Kobayashi, T. & Kitamura, T. (1998). Duration modeling for HMM-based speech synthesis, *Proc. of ICSLP*, pp. 29–32.

Yoshimura, T., Tokuda, K., Masuko, T., Kobayashi, T. & Kitamura, T. (1997). Speaker interpolation in HMM-based speech synthesis system, *Proc. of Eurospeech*, pp. 2523–2526.

Yoshimura, T., Tokuda, K., Masuko, T., Kobayashi, T. & Kitamura, T. (1999). Simultaneous modeling of spectrum, pitch and duration in HMM-based speech synthesis, *Proc. of Eurospeech*, pp. 2347–2350.

Z-H. Ling, K., Richmond, J. Y. & Wang, R.-H. (2009). Integrating articulatory features into HMM-based parametric speech synthesis, *IEEE Trans. Audio, Speech, Lang. Process.* 17(6): 1171–1185.

Zen, H., Tokuda, K. & Black, A. W. (2009). Statistical parametric speech synthesis, *Speech Commun.* 51(11): 1039–1064.

Zen, H., Tokuda, K., Masuko, T., Kobayashi, T. & Kitamura, T. (2004). Hidden semi-Markov model based speech synthesis, *Proc. of Interspeech*, pp. 1393–1396.

6

Automatic Visual Speech Recognition

Alin Chiţu[1] and Léon J.M. Rothkrantz[1,2]

[1]Delft University of Technology
[2]Netherlands Defence Academy
The Netherlands

1. Introduction

Lip reading was thought for many years to be specific to hearing impaired persons. Therefore, it was considered that lip reading is one possible solution to an abnormal situation. Even the name of the domain suggests that lip reading was considered to be a rather artificial way of communication because it associates lip reading with the written language which is a relatively new cultural phenomenon and is not an evolutionary inherent ability. Extensive lip reading research was primarily done in order to improve the teaching methodology for hearing impaired persons to increase their chances for integration in the society. Later on, the research done in human perception and more exactly in speech perception proved that lip reading is actively employed in different degrees by all humans irrespective to their hearing capacity. The most well know study in this respect was performed by Harry McGurk and John MacDonald in 1976. In their experiment the two researchers were trying to understand the perception of speech by children. Their finding, now called the McGurk effect, published in Nature (Mcgurk & Macdonald, 1976), was that if a person is presented a video sequence with a certain utterance (i.e. in their experiments utterance 'ga'), but in the same time the acoustics present a different utterance (i.e. in their experiments the sound 'ba'), in a large majority of cases the person will perceive a third utterance (i.e. in this case 'da'). Subsequent experiments showed that this is true as well for longer utterances and that is not a particularity of the visual and aural senses but also true for other perception functions. Therefore, lip reading is part of our multi-sensory speech perception process and could be better named visual speech recognition. Being an evolutionary acquired capacity, same as speech perception, some scientists consider the lip reading's neural mechanism the one that enables humans to achieve high literacy skills with relative easiness (van Atteveldt, 2006).

Another source of confusion is the "lip" word, because it implies that the lips are the only part of the speaker face that transmit information about what is being said. The teeth, the tongue and the cavity were shown to be of great importance for lip reading by humans (Williams et al., 1998). Also other face elements were shown to be important during face to face communication; however, their exact influence is not completely elucidated. During experiments in which a gaze tracker was used to track the speaker's areas of attention during communication it was found that the human lip readers focus on four major areas: the mouth, the eyes and the centre of the face depending on the task and the noise level (Buchan et al., 2007). In normal situations the listener scans the mouth and the other areas relatively equal periods of times. However, when the background noise increases, the centre of the face becomes the central point of attention. Most probably the peripheral vision becomes extremely active in these situations. When the task was set to the inference of the emotional load of the interlocutor, the listener's gaze started to be shifted towards the eyes since they convey more emotional related information. It is well accepted that the human lip readers make great use of the context in which the interaction takes place. This can be one of the reasons the human listener scans the entire face during the interaction. In (Hilder et al., 2009) the authors found that when a human lip reader was presented with appearance information, compared with only mouth shapes, his performance increased considerably from 42.9% to 71.6%.

We should realise that during face to face interaction a human engages in a complex process which involves various channels of information corresponding to our senses. In this way the speaker builds up the context using both verbal and non-verbal cues such as body gesture, facial expressions, prosody, and other physiological manifestations. Other information about the settings in which the communication takes place is used as well as the knowledge accumulated in time through experience. A human is a multi-modality, multi-sensory, multi-media fusing machine.

The rest of the chapter is organized as follows: section 2 presents relevant research works in the area of lip reading. Section 3 presents the aspects related to building an automated lip reader. Section 4 details the characteristics of the facial model used during the visual analysis of the lip reading process. The next sections illustrate the results and discuss the conclusions of the algorithms presented in the chapter.

2. State of the art in lip reading

It is about three decades since automatic lip reading domain emerged in the scientific community. However, only starting from the 90s, and more sustained in the second half of the 90s, the subject started to become viable. Even today it still lags the speech recognition by some decades. Until some years ago the most impeding factor was the computational power of the computers. Nowadays it is the difficulty in finding the most suitable visual features that capture the information related with what is being spoken. Also it is the hard problem of accurately detecting and tracking the facial elements that convey speech related information. The automatic and robust detection and tracking of the face elements is still not entirely achieved by the current technology. As in other similar visual pattern recognition applications, the two monsters "illumination variations" and "occlusions" are still alive and menacing. A special case of occlusion is in this case generated by the posture of the speaker.

Therefore, any study concerning lip reading deals with the overwhelming task of manually or in the best case semi-automatically processing the data corpus. The data corpora for lip reading are still very small due to partially the storage and bandwidth limitations and other recording related settings, but much more limiting due to the overwhelming task of processing and preparing the data for experiments. Because of these issues, each data corpus is created for a stated recognition task. The lip reading experiments to this date are limited to isolated or connected random words, isolated or connected digits, isolated or connected letters. Some of the reported performance is listed below. However, it is very important to keep in mind that, because the data corpus used influences in great respect the performance of the lip reader, a comparison among the experiments is not always possible. When the corpora are about the same, then the comparison of the different feature types and feature extraction techniques becomes feasible. It can still give an impression on the state of the art in lip reading.

The task of isolated letters was among the first analysed by Petajan et al. (Petajan et al., 1988) back in 1998. The authors report the correct recognition close to 90%. However, based on the AVletters data corpus, Matthews et al. (Matthews et al., 1996) reports only a 50% recognition rate. Li et al. (Li et al., 1995) reports a perfect recognition 100% on the same task, but two years later in (Li et al., 1997) only 90% recognition. The second most popular task is digit recognition either in isolation or as connected strings. Based on the TULIPS1 data corpus, which only contains the first four digits, Luettin et al. (Luettin et al., 1996) and Luettin and Thacker (Luettin & Thacker, 1997) reported 83.3% and 88.5% recognition rates, respectively. Arsic and Thiran (Arsic & Thiran, 2006) report on the same data corpus 81.25% and 89.6% depending on the feature extraction method. Other experiments with the digit recognition task are: Potamianos et al. (Potamianos et al., 1998) reported 95.7%, Dupont and Luettin (Dupont & Luettin, 2000) reported 59.7%, Wojdel reported in his thesis (Wojdel, 2003) 91.1% correct recognition and 81.1% accuracy, Patamianos et al. (Potamianos et al., 2004) reported 63% and Perez et al. (Prez et al., 2005) 47%. Lucey and Potamianos (Lucey & Potamianos, 2006) reported 74.6% recognition rate for the isolated digits task. Potamianos et al. (Potamianos1998a) report 64.5% recognition rate for the connected letter task. For the isolated word task Nefian et al. (Nefian et al., 2002) report 66.9%, Zhang et al. (Zhang et al., 2002) report 42%, Kumar et al. (Kumar et al., 2007) report 42.3%. We can conclude that there is still a large variation in the performances obtained, and there is still no convergence visible since the newer studies do not necessarily show an increase in accuracy. This is, to our opinion, clearly a sign of the immaturity of the lip reading domain. Also, as can be observed in the listing above, there are yet no results of experiments with continuous speech. Patamianos et al. (Potamianos et al., 2004) report an extremely low result on the continuous speech task, namely 12%. The lip reading domain is still young and there are many limiting factors that need to be conquered. Therefore, the experiments in lip reading are still dealing with relatively easy tasks. However, the promising results in these tasks give us hopes that larger experiments are possible. As the domain becomes more popular, the number of data corpora will increase and with a better cooperation among scientists it will be possible to better compare the achievements. However, there are objective factors which limit the performance of the lip readers. Nevertheless, as shown in many studies, lip reading can be successfully used in conjunction with speech for an enhanced speech recognition system.

3. Building an automatic lip reader: Overview

Building a lip reader is in many ways similar to building any automatic system which performs an autonomous role in its environment. The first decision needed to be made before starting the construction of the system is with respect to the role of the system and with respect to the environment where the system will be deployed. After establishing, in pattern recognition jargon, the recognition task, building the system consists of four separate stages: data acquisition, data parametrization, model training and model testing. Figure 1 describes the general process of building a lip reader. These activities are performed in cycles, the larger the cycle the less frequent its corresponding process is performed.

The data acquisition process should ensure that the resulting corpus correctly describes the distribution of the possible states of the modelled process. The importance of the data parametrization is twofold; it should extract only the relevant information from the data and it should reduce the dimensionality of the feature space, therefore increasing the tractability of the problem. Training and testing are dependent on the mathematical models chosen for inference. These range from plain heuristics to complex probabilistic graphical models. The training process should solve two problems: identify the structure of the models such as the number of parameters and their relation, and compute the values of the models' parameters.

Training and testing is usually performed in a cycle which will fine tune the structure of the models and the values of the weights in the model. However, the data parametrization step is the one that is most of the time investigated, since there are many ways to extract suitable information for the process under study. Choosing the right parametrization is not straightforward and usually a trial and error sequence of experiments is started.

Fig. 1. The activity sequence for building a lip reader

A lip reader and in general a speech recogniser is built for a particular target language. The recognition task, namely the size of the vocabulary and the type of utterances accepted, are paramount for the entire design of the system. For instance if for a small vocabulary (i.e. a few tens of words) one model can be used to recognise one entire word, for larger vocabularies it is more suitable to build sub-word models, i.e., to directly recognise sub-words and build the words and sentences using dictionaries and grammar networks.

So far, the most successful approach for speech recognition, and therefore also applied to lip reading, is the Bayesian approach. In the Bayesian approach, the recognition problem can be formulated as follows: given a set of possible words and an observation sequence $O = (O_1, O_2, ..., O_n)$ the solution of the recognition problem is the word that maximizes the probability $P(W|O)$. Based on the Bayesian rule we can write: $P(W|O) = \dfrac{P(O|W)P(W)}{P(O)}$, where $P(O|W)$ is the likelihood of the observation given the word W and P (W), usually called the language model, represents the probability of the word W. The problem can be thus rewritten as: $\hat{W} = argmax_W (P(O|W)P(W))$, where W is the recognized word. In the above equation the denominator $P(O)$ has been deleted since it does not influence the solution. Therefore, the recognition problem is reduced to building a language model P(W) and a word model $P(O|W)$ for each legal word.

3.1 On building a data corpus for lip reading: A comparison

In order to evaluate the results of different solutions to a certain problem, the data corpora used should be shared between researchers or otherwise there should exist a set of guidelines for building a corpus that all datasets should comply with. In the case when a data corpus is build with the intention to be made public, a greater level of reusability is required. In all cases, the first and probably the most important step in building a data corpus is to carefully state the targeted applications of the system that will be trained using the dataset. Some of the most cited data corpora for lip reading are: TULIPS1 (Movellan, 1995), AVletters (Matthews et al., 1996), AVOZES (Goecke & Millar, 2004), CUAVE (Patterson et al., 2002), DAVID (Chibelushi et al., 1996), ViaVoice (Neti et al., 2000), DUTAVSC (Wojdel et al., 2002), AVICAR (Lee et al., 2004), AT&T (Potamianos et al., 1997), CMU (Zhang et al., 2002), XM2VTSDB (Messer et al., 1999), M2VTS (Pigeon & Vandendorpe, 1997) and LIUM-AVS (Daubias & Deleglise, 2003). With the exception of M2VTS which is in French, XM2VTSDB which is in four languages and DUTAVSC which is in Dutch the rest are only in English (Table 1). Since the target language for our research was Dutch, we had only one option, namely the DUTAVSC (Delft University of Technology Audio-Visual Speech Corpus). For reasons that will be explained in the next paragraphs, we decided to build our own data corpus. This corpus was build as an extension to the DUTAVSC and is called NDUTAVSC (Chitu & Rothkrantz, 2009) which stands for "New Delft University of Technology Audio-Visual Speech Corpus".

Some aspects related to the data set preparation are as follows:

- The complexity of audio data recording is much smaller than of the video recordings. Therefore, all datasets store the audio signal with sufficiently high accuracy, namely using a sample rate of 22 kHz to 48 kHz and a sample size of 16 bits. Therefore, the quality of the audio data is not subject to storage accuracy but from the perspective of recording environment. There are two approaches to the recordings environment: specific and neutral. In the first case the database is built with a very narrow application domain in mind such as speech recognition in the car. In this case the recording environment matches the conditions of the environment where the system will be deployed. This approach can guarantee that the particularities of the target environment are closely matched. The downside of this approach is that the resulting corpus is too much dedicated to the problem domain and suffers from over training, and offers little generalization. In the second approach the dataset can be recorded in controlled, noise free environment. The advantage of this approach is the possibility to adapt the corpus to a specific environment in a post process. Therefore, a data corpus of this kind can be used for virtually any number of applications. The specific noise can be simulated or recorded in the required conditions and later superimposed on the clear audio data.
- In the case of video data recording there is a larger number of important factors that control the success of the resulting data corpus. Hence, not only the environment, but also the equipment used for recording and other settings is actively influencing the final result. In the case of the environment the classification made for audio holds for video as well. The environment where the recordings are made is important since it can determine the illumination of the scene, and the background of the speakers. In the case of a controlled environment the speakers background is usually monochrome so that by

using a "colour keying" technique the speaker can be placed in different locations inducing in this way some degree of visual noise. However, the illumination conditions of different environment are not as easily applied to the clean recordings, since the 3D information is not available anymore. In controlled environments the light is reflected by special panels which cast the light uniformly, reducing the artefacts on the speaker's faces.

- The equipment used for recording plays a major role, because the resolution and the sample rate is still a heavy burden. Hence, the resolution of the recordings ranges from 100x75 pixels in Tulips1 and 80x60 pixels in AVletters datasets to 720x576 pixels in AVOZES and CUAVE datasets. The same improvement in quality is also observed in colour fidelity.

- The frame rate of the existing data corpora is conforming to one of the colour encoding systems used in broadcast television systems. Therefore, the video is recorded at 24Hz, 25Hz, 29.97Hz of 30Hz depending on the place in the world where the recordings are made. The data corpus used for the current research was recorded at 100Hz.

- The Region Of Interest (ROI) is important as well. For lip reading only the lower half of the face is important. However, in case context information is required, a larger area might be needed. Most of the datasets show, however, a passport like image of the speaker. In our opinion, at least for increasing the performance of the parametrization process a smaller ROI is more advantageous. Of course a ROI that is too narrow adds high constraints on the performances of the video camera used and it might be argued that this is not the case in real life where the resulting system will be used. Recording only the mouth area as is done in the Tulips1 data set is a tough goal to achieve in an uncontrolled environment. However, by using a face detection algorithm combined with a face tracking algorithm we could automatically focus and zoom in on the face of the speaker. A small ROI facilitates acquiring a much greater detail of the area of interest, in our case the mouth area, while keeping the resolution and, therefore, the bandwidth needs in manageable limits.

Figure 2 shows some examples from six available data corpora. The differences among the examples in this figure are clearly visible, with the exception of the DUTAVSC corpus, all other corpora reserve a small number of pixels for the mouth area. Table 2 gives the sizes of the mouth bounding box in all six samples. This low level of detail makes the detection and tracking of the lips much more difficult. Any parametrization that considers a description of the shape of the mouth will be heavily influenced by image degradation. In the paper

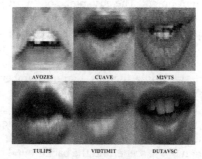

Fig. 2. The resolution of the ROI in some data corpora available for lip reading

(Potamianos et al., 1998) the authors report that the degradation of the video signal by the image compression algorithm by the addition of white noise does not influence the lip reading performance unless the Signal to Noise Ratio(SNR) falls under some threshold: 50% and 15%, respectively. These findings are reported when the features used are a linear transformation of the intensities in the images, namely discrete wavelet transform.

Corpus	Language	Sessions	Respondents	Audio Quality	Video Quality	Language Quality	Stated purpose
TULIPS1	English	1	7male, 5female	11.1kHz, 8bits controlled audio	100x75, 8bit, 30fps mouth region	first 4 digits in English	small vocabulary isolated words recognition
AVletters	English	1	5male, 5female	22kHz, 16bits controlled audio	80x60, 8buts, 25fps mouth region	the English alphabet	spelling English alphabet
AVOZES	English	1	10male, 10female	48kHz, 16bits controlled audio	720x480, 24bits, 29.97fps entire face, stereo view	digits from '0' to '9' continuous speech application driven utterances	continuous speech recognition for Australian English
CUAVE	English	1	19male, 17female	44kHz, 16bits controlled audio	720x480, 24bits 29.970fps passport view	7,000 utterances connected and isolated digits	continuous speech recognition
Vid-TIMIT	English	3	24male, 19female	32kHz, 16bits controlled audio	512x384, 24bits, 25fps upper body	TIMIT corpus 10 sentences per person	automatic lipreading, face recognition
DAVID	English	12	132male, 126female (in 4 groups)	--	entire face, upper body, profile view multi corpora: controlled and degraded background, highlighted lips	vowel – consonants alternation. English digits	speech or person recognition
IBM LVCSR*	English	1	290 Unknown gender	22kHz, 16bits --	--	connected digits isolated words	audio-visual speech recognition
AVICAR	English	5	50male, 50female	48kHz, 16bits, 8channels 5 levels of noise car specific	4 cameras from different angles, passport view car environment	isolated digits, isolated letters, connected digits, TIMIT sentences	speech recognition in a car environment
DUTAVSC	Dutch	10-14	7male, 1female	48kHz, 16bits, controlled audio	384x288, 24bits, 25fps lower face view	spelling, connected digits, application driven utterances, POLYPHONE corpus**	audio-visual speech recognition, lipreading

* Not available to the public
** Data corpus for Dutch. Recordings are made over phone lines. More details can be found in (Damhuis et al. 1994)

Table 1. Characteristics of data corpora.

Data corpus	Width	Height
AVOZES	122	24
CUAVE	75	34
M2VTS	46	28
TULIPS1	76	37
VidTIMIT	53	25
DUTAVSC	225	133

Table 2. Resolution of the mouth area in six known corpora for lip reading.

3.1.1 Language quality

By its nature lip reading requires, irrespective of the other qualities, that the data corpus has a good coverage of the language and task vocabulary. Therefore, in the case of a word based recognizer all the words in the vocabulary need to be present in the corpus. In the case of a sub-word recognizer every sub-word item needs to be present in the corpus in all existing contexts. Therefore, the co-articulatory effects appear with a reasonable frequency. However, due to the amount of work necessary and the storage and bandwidth required most of the data corpora only consider small recognition tasks and small language corpus. Most frequently the data corpora focus on the digits and letters of the language considered. These are recorded either isolated, or in short sequences, or as in DUTAVSC in spelling of words. Some corpora even only consider nonsense combinations of vowels(V) and consonants(C) (e.g. DAVID considers VCVCVC sequences, AVOZES repetitions of "ba" and "eo" constructions, AT&T CVC sequences). The continuous speech case is only considered in AVOZES which contains only 3 phonetically balanced sentences, in AVICAR which contains ten sentences from the TIMIT (Garofolo, 1988) speech data corpus, XM2VTSDB and M2VTS which contains one random sentence and DUTAVSC which contains 80 phonetically rich sentences. The DUTAVSC is by far the most rich data corpus. The NDUTAVSC corpus which was built as an extension of DUTAVSC contains more than 2000 unique rich sentences. However, none of the existing corpora can match the language coverage offered by the data corpora used for speech recognition which can easily have a vocabulary of 100k words (e.g. the Polyphone corpus (Boogaart et al., 1994) contains more than one million words recorded and a vocabulary of 150k words).

3.2 Feature vectors definition

There are many approaches to data parametrization, but with respect to the feature vectors definition they all fit in three broad classes: texture based features, geometric based features, and combination of texture and geometric features. A good overview of most of the feature extraction methods can be found in (Potamianos et al., 2004). In the first class the feature vectors are composed of pixels' intensities values or a transformation of them in some smaller feature space. The main function of the projection is to reduce the dimensionality of the feature space while preserving as much as possible the most relevant speech related information. Principal Component Analysis (PCA) is one of the first choices, and therefore very popular, and was used in many studies e.g. (Bregler et al., 1993); (Bregler & Konig, 1994); (Duchnowski et al., 1994); (Li et al., 1995); (Tomlinson et al., 1996); (Chiou & Hwang, 1997); (Gray et al., 1997); (Li et al., 1997); (Luettin & Thacker, 1997); (Potamianos et al., 1998); (Dupont & Luettin, 2000); (Hong et al., 2006). The feature definition is based on the notion of eigenfaces or eigenlips which represent the eigenvectors of the training sets. An alternative to PCA, very common as well, is Discrete Cosine Transform (DCT) such as in (Duchnowski et al., 1995); (Prez et al., 2005); (Hong et al., 2006); (Lucey & Potamianos, 2006). Linear Discriminant Analysis (LDA), Maximum Likelihood Data Rotation (MLLT), Discrete Wavelet Transform, Discrete Walsh Transform (Potamianos et al., 1998) are other methods that fit in this class and were used for lip reading. Virtually, any other method, usually borrowed from the data compression domain, which results in a lower dimensionality of the feature vectors can be applied for data parametrization in the lip reading domain. Local Binary Patterns (LBP) is just another technique, borrowed from the texture segmentation domain, and shows promising results for lip reading as well (Morn & Pinto-Elas, 2007); (Zhao et al., 2007); (Kricke et al., 2008). LBP was developed by Timo Ojala and Matti Pietikainen and presented in (Ojala & Pietikainen, 1997). A special place in this class is taken by the feature vectors that are based on Optical Flow Analysis (OFA) (Mase & Pentland, 1991); (Martin, 1995); (Gray et al., 1997); (Fleet et al., 2000); (Iwano et al., 2001); (Tamura et al., 2002); (Furui, 2003); (Yoshinaga et al., 2003); (Yoshinaga et al., 2004); (Tamura et al., 2004); (Chitu et al., 2007); (Chitu & Rothkrantz, 2009). The optical flow is defined as "the apparent velocity field in an image". This definition closely matches the affirmation of

Bregler and Konig in their 1994 paper (Bregler & Konig, 1994): "The real information in lipreading lies in the temporal change of lip positions, rather than the absolute lip shape". The OFA can be used as well as a measure of the overall movement and be employed for onset/offset detection. The main advantage of this approach is that it can be easily automated, since it requires only the definition of the Region Of Interest (ROI). The ROI can be considered the bounding box of the face or the bounding box of the mouth, thus requiring some object detection and tracking algorithm. A good example is the face detection algorithm developed by Viola and Jones in (Viola & Jones, 2001). The main disadvantage of this type of features is that the a-priory information about lip reading is not inherently used in the process of feature extraction. Therefore, there is minimum control over the information contained in the resulting feature vectors, on whether this information is relevant for lip reading or not. The exceptions can be the OPA and LBP where the analysis is usually performed in carefully chosen regions around the mouth. We defined the set of features based on OFA and analyzed the performance of the lip reading system trained on our data corpus. The features from the second class share the belief that in order to accurately capture the most relevant features, with respect to lip reading, a careful description of the contour of the speaker's mouth is needed. The feature extraction proceeds in two steps; first a number of key points are detected and based on these points the mouth contour is recovered, and second the feature vectors are defined based on the shape of the mouth. The detection of the key points is performed based on colour segmentation techniques that identify pixels that are on the lips. Thereafter, the contour of the lips is usually extracted by imposing a lip model to the detected points. These methods are using the so called "smart snakes" (Lievin et al., 1999); (Luettin & Thacker, 1997); (Salazar et al., 2007), or as called in (Eveno et al., 2004) "jumping snakes", or later on Active Shape Models (ASM) (Luettin et al., 1996); (Prez et al., 2005); (Morn & Pinto-Elas, 2007) or Active Contour Models (ACM). Any other parametric model can be used here. The lips' contour is usually detected as a result of an iterative process which searches to minimise the error between the real contour and the approximation of the contour the parametric model allows for. The actual feature vectors are defined in the second step. The feature vectors fall into two categories here: model based features and mouth high level features. In the first category the feature vectors contain directly the parameters of the models used for describing the mouth contour. In the second category the feature vectors contain measurable quantities, which are meaningful to humans. The most used high level features are mouth height, mouth width, contour perimeter, aperture height, aperture width, aperture area, mouth area, aperture angle and other relations among these (e.g. the ratio between the width and the height) (Chitu & Rothkrantz, 2009); (Goecke et al., 2000a, 2000b); (Kumar et al., 2007); (Matthews et al., 2002); (Yoshinaga et al., 2004).

In our research we used Statistical Lip Geometry Estimation (LGE) which is a feature extraction method introduced by Wojdel and Rothkrantz (Wojdel & Rothkrantz, 2000). This method is special because it is a model free approach for describing the shape of the lips. It strongly depends, however, on the performance of the image segmentation technique used to detect the pixels which belong to the lips. The third class consists of feature vectors that contain both geometric and texture features. The features from each category are usually concatenated in a larger feature vector. For instance (Dupont & Luettin, 2000) and (Luettin et al., 1996) combine ASM with PCA features and (Chiou & Hwang, 1997) combines snake features with PCA. It was shown that the tongue, teeth and cavity have great influence on lip reading (Williams et al., 1998), therefore, the addition of these appearance related elements has significant influence on the performance of lip reading (Chitu et al., 2007). A special example is the so called Active Appearance Models (AAM) (Cootes et al., 1998) which combines the ASM method with texture based information to accurately detect the shape of the mouth or the face. The searching algorithm is iteratively adjusting the shape such that to minimise the error between the generated shape and the real shape. The core of AAM is PCA which is applied three times, on the shape space, on the texture space and on the combined space of shape and texture. The AAM based features can either consist of AAM model parameters in which case we have a combined geometric and texture feature vector, or of high level features computed based on the shape generated in which case we have a geometric feature vector. The lip reading results based on high level feature vectors which are computed starting from the lips' shape generated based on AAM are given in this chapter.

3.3 Lip reading primitives

This section introduces the visemes which are the lip reading counterparts of the phonemes.

3.3.1 Phonemes

In any spoken language a phoneme is the smallest segmental unit of sound which generates a meaningful contrast between utterances. Thus a phoneme is a group of slightly different sounds which are all perceived to have the same function by speakers of the language or dialect in question. An example of a phoneme is the group of /p/ sounds in the words pit spin and tip. Even though these /p/ sounds are formed differently and are slightly different sounds they belong to the same phoneme in English because for an English speaker interchanging the sounds will not change the meaning of the word, however strange the word will sound. The phones, or sounds, that make up a phoneme are called allophones. A speech recognizer can be built at word level or at sub-word level. While for a small vocabulary recognition task a word level system might be preferred, for large vocabulary, continuous speech task systems the phonemes are used as building blocks. Therefore, each phoneme in the target language corresponds to a recognition model in the speech recognizer.

In the Dutch language, approximately 40 distinguishable phonemes are defined. However, there can be slight differences among different phoneme and phoneme sets as a consequence of the target dialect and definition of accepted words. In the present research we used the phoneme set defined in (Damhuis et al., 1994). One problem is generated, for instance, by the neologisms. These words are divided in two classes: the ones that are already established into the language (e.g. the words of French origin) and have a stable pronunciation but which contain phonemes that are still under-represented in the language and a second class of very new words (e.g. the International English words from various technical and economical background) which bring a set of new phonemes that have no correspondence in Dutch. Table 3 shows the phonemes of the Dutch language as used in the Polyphone corpus. The phonemes are given in International Phonetic Alphabet (IPA), Speech Assessment Methods Phonetic Alphabet (SAMPA), and HTK notations, respectively.

3.3.2 From phonemes to visemes

Even though the definition of the concept of phoneme crosses the boundary of the auditory realm, and therefore is not bound to any sensory modality, the term "viseme" is used as the counter part of phoneme in the visual modality. The term was introduced by Fisher in (Fisher, 1968).

The visemes have a similar definition with the phonemes, namely, a viseme is a set of indistinguishable phonemes; indistinguishable phonemes from the point of view of the visual information available and not as in the phonemes case from the point of view of their meaning. There are two direct consequences of this definition. Firstly, there is no exact method of deciding the number and composition of the viseme classes; this is actually done either by a theoretical discussion of auditory-visual lip reading of phonemes or by modelling the human ability of recognizing the phonemes in the absence of the auditory stimulus, therefore, by modelling the degree of confusion of phonemes in the visual modality. Secondly, since there is no one-to-one mapping between the phonetic transcription of an utterance and the corresponding visual transcription, the separability of utterances in the visual modality decreases, which decreases the theoretical performance of a lip reader. The dependence of the visemes on the phonemes can be thought of as one reason why a new term was needed.

Unlike for English, to date there is only a limited number of publications which deal with the definition of visemes in Dutch; this is an almost complete list of them: (Breeuwer, 1985), (Corthals , 1984), (Eggermont, 1964), (van Son et al., 1994), (Visser et al., 1999) and (Beun, 1996). The papers (van Son et al., 1994) and (Beun, 1996) cited in (Wojdel, 2003), are the only examples, at least to the author's knowledge, where the classification of the viseme sets is done by elicitation of the human confusion matrices of phonemes. The authors of (van Son et al., 1994) found in their experiments that the Dutch lip readers are only able to recognize four consonantal and four vocalic visemes.

3.3.3 Modelling the visemes using HMM

As a sub-word based speech recogniser, the building blocks of our lip reader are the visemes of the Dutch language. Therefore, one HMM corresponds to one viseme. To the set of visemes are added two special models, namely sp for "short pause" and sil for "silence". The sp model is used for recognition of the short pause between words, while sil is used for the silence moments before and after the utterance. Depending on the recognition task, some visemes do not appear at all in the expected utterances and are, therefore, excluded from the study. This is the case for the digit and letter tasks.

The set of visemes which appear in the digit recognition task are listed in Table 4 and the set of visemes which appear in the letter recognition task are listed in Table 5. The visemes "at" and "a" are only present in the digit set, while the visemes "aa" and "pbm" are only present in the letter set.

The topology of the models used for modelling the visemes, usually used for phoneme-based speech recognition as well, is a 3-state left-right with no skips as shown in Figure 3. For implementation reasons, HTK requires that the models start and end with a non emitting node that facilitate the generation of recognition networks. A recognition network consists of a string of linked models which are used during recognition by matching to the input utterance.

	Symbol			Example Word		
	IPA	SAMPA	HTK	Orthography	Transcription	Translation
1	p	p	p	pak	p a k	package
2	b	b	b	bak	b a k	container
3	t	t	t	tak	t a k	branch
4	d	d	d	dak	d a k	roof
5	k	k	k	kat	k a t	cat
6	g	g	gg	goal	gg oo l	goal(sports)
7	f	f	f	fel	f e l	fierce
8	v	v	v	vel	v e l	sheet
9	s	s	s	sein	s ei n	signal
10	z	z	z	zijn	z ei n	to be
11	x	x	x	acht	a x t	eight
12	ɣ	G	g	negen	n ee g at	nine
13	ɦ	h	h	hand	h a n t	hand
14	ʒ	Z	zj	bagage	b a g aa zj at	luggage
15	ʃ	S	sh	sjaal	sh aa l	scarf
16	m	m	m	met	m e t	with
17	n	n	n	nek	n e k	neck
18	ŋ	N	nn	bang	b a nn	scared
19	l	l	l	land	l a n t	country
20	r	R	r	rand	r a n t	edge
21	ʋ	w	w	wit	w i t	white
22	j	j	j	ja	j a	yes

Table 3. Polyphone's Dutch phoneme set: consonants.

	Viseme			Viseme
1	gkx	8		ei
2	oyu	9		sz
3	l	10		eeh
4	iee	11		at
5	td	12		a
6	fvw	13		sil
7	ie	14		sp

Table 4. The viseme set in HTK working notation for the digit recognition task.

	Viseme			Viseme
1	aa	9		h
2	pbm	10		ie
3	iee	11		ei
4	sz	12		l
5	td	13		oyu
6	eeh	14		sil
7	fvw	15		sp
8	gkx			

Table 5. The viseme set in HTK working notation for the letter recognition task.

In Figure 3 the numbers on the arcs represent the initial transition probabilities, set before training. Under the emitting states there is a generic drawing of the distribution of the feature vectors which is approximated by a mixture of Gaussian distributions. The modelling of the two silence models are introduced in the next section.

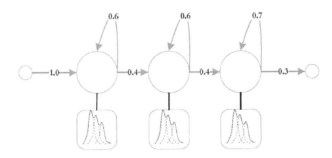

Fig. 3. The models used for modelling the visemes. The topology is 5-State Left-Right with three emitting states. The arcs are annotated with transition probabilities

3.3.4 Silence and pause models

It is not possible to build a continuous speech recognizer without including a model for silence. However, there are two types of silence, the ones between the words and the ones that appear in the beginning of the utterance and at the end of the utterance. The silence model that covers the entering and exit time of the utterances can be modelled using the same topology as for viseme models (i.e. 3-state left-right topology). However, in order to make the model more robust by allowing the states to absorb more non verbal mouth movement, the silence model is modified so that a backwards transition from state 4 to state 2 is accepted. The model for short pause is build starting from the model for [sil]. The short pause model is a so called tee-model and has a single emitting state which is tied to the central state of the [sp] model. This means that the central state of the [sil] model and the emitting state of the [sp] model share the same Gaussian mixture and therefore are trained using the same data. Parameter tying is very often used in speech recognition for the cases when there is not sufficient data for training models for similar entities. The topology used for the two silence models is shown in Figure 4. The silence models defined above are the same as the ones used for speech recognition. However, there is a big difference between the concept of silence in speech recognition and the concept of silence in lip reading. Consequently, the noise can have a more robust definition. For instance, in the case of visual speech the speaker can move his mouth for non verbal reasons (e.g. to moisture his lips, or to exteriorise the emotional status by showing a facial expression). The noise sources are more diverse for lip reading. Even though the silence model has an extra backward arc which should, in principle, also accommodate for noise in the training data, we found out in our experiments that the silence model defined in this way did not perform at the same level as in the case of speech. As we will see later in the results sections, sometimes the insertion rate was unexpectedly large. This can also be due to poorly trained silence models.

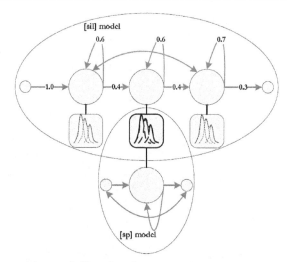

Fig. 4. The models used for modelling the silence

3.3.5 Modelling the low level context using Tri-visemes

In order to model the context at the level of the visemes, each viseme is considered in all the possible contexts. Only a one step context is considered, namely for each viseme only the left and the right possible visemes are considered, therefore, the name of the new entity is tri-viseme. The notation for tri-visemes is lf-vis+rt, where "vis" is the viseme in question, "lf" is the left context and "rt" is right context. For instance the word nul with the viseme transcription gkx oyu l will generate the following tri-visemes: gkx+oyu, gkx-oyu+l and oyu-l. The context of each viseme can be build at word level, also called word internal, or at the level of utterance called word external. In the first case, for finding all possible contexts of a viseme, only the words in the vocabulary are considered, while in the second case also the possible combinations of words can build the context. It should be noted that sometimes bi-visemes (i.e. viseme context containing only the left or the right viseme) are also generated. For each tri-viseme, a new model will be build which makes the number of models explode, making the data requirements for training a tri-viseme based recognizer many times larger. The major problem with the tri-visemes is that some contexts can appear only once (or a very small number of times) in the training data, or can even be absent from the training data, as in the case of trans-word boundary contexts. To solve this problem the parameter tying technique is used. The clustering of possible similar contexts can be made either by a data-driven approach, or by the use of decision trees. Even after the parameter tying, there can still be tri-viseme models which are undertrained.

3.4 Gaussian mixtures

The HMM approach considers that each of the emitting states in the model will be described by a continuous density distribution. This distribution is approximated in HTK by a mixture of Gaussian distributions. Building of the models in HTK starts by using only one Gaussian distribution. In the refining step the number of Gaussian mixtures is increased iteratively by 1 or 2 units until the optimum number of components is obtained. By monitoring the performance change, the optimum number of mixtures can be found. During our experiments we iteratively increased the number of mixtures by one until a maximum of 32 mixtures. The "magic" number 32 was found sufficiently big to cover the optimum number of mixtures in all the experiments.

4. Facial model for lip reading

The AAM algorithm iteratively searches for the best fit of a model defined by a set of landmarks and the image being processed. Based on a-priori knowledge about the shape of the object, the set of landmarks is defined such that it optimally describes the object. In our case we required that the points selected describe the shape of the mouth in detail, especially capturing the speech related aspects. Therefore, the final model should exactly segment the lips in all moments during speech. After experimenting with different models and analysing the results, followed by long discussions, we decided to use a model composed of 29 points, distributed around the mouth, chin and nose. This model is shown in Figure 5.

For training a model, a number of two to four hundred images was manually processed. In order to obtain reliable results the images were selected such that they cover all the variance in the data. This was achieved in an iterative process. We first started with a random selection of a few tens of images which were used to build a first model. This model was used for processing until the performance of the model decreased below some visually assessed threshold. The images that were badly processed were added in the training set and a new model was obtained. This process continued until the performance of the model stabilized. In the end we trained a number of models for each speaker in the dataset. For speakers that recorded multiple sessions we trained one model per session.

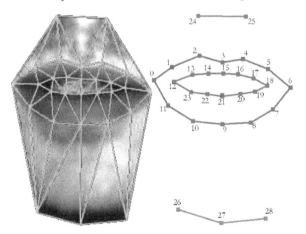

Fig. 5. The AAM model

Even though the process is fairly automated, this was an extremely laborious work, since the corpus contains more than 4.3 million frames, and was split among various people. Each assistant was asked to train a model and supervise the processing of the rest of the frames. Splitting the data among different people makes it more difficult to guaranty the uniformity over the entire corpus of the end result. Therefore, to assure uniformity of the processing we used a strict definition of the landmarks. We defined as well constraints that acted on pairs of landmarks. The rest of this section gives the definition used for the landmarks. Before going to the next paragraphs, we should introduce some anatomical elements on which the definition of the landmarks depends.

4.1 AAM results on the training data

The AAM process is very fast and very accurate given that a good training set was selected. We combined the AAM searching scheme with the Viola&Jones mouth detection algorithm, which made the selection of a very good location for the initial guess possible. This has speeded up the search process to real time performance. The mouth detection was used only in the first few frames of the recording. In the subsequent frames the initial guess used was the result of the processing in the previous frame. This approach was very successful both in speeding up the search scheme and improving the accuracy of the detection. Figure 6 shows the first six most important components in PCA terminology. The mean shape and texture model is shown on the centre row. The top row shows for each mode the resulting object after an adjustment by two standard deviations is applied to on the corresponding mode. The bottom row shows the result when the adjustment is negative. The first two modes seem to have more control over the vertical and horizontal movement of the mouth, while mode four seems to control the presence of the tongue. However, there is no strict separation between the information controlled by each mode, at least not easily discernable by visual inspection. This model was trained on a set of 440 images, selected in an iterative process. All three models (i.e. appearance, shape and combined models) were truncated at 95% level. Based on the 95% level truncation, the final combined model had 38 parameters, while the shape model had 11 parameters and the texture model had 120 parameters. The first six modes in the combined model cover 78.65%. However, in the case of the shape models the first two modes already cover 82.53% of the total variation, while the first six cover 91.83% of the variation.

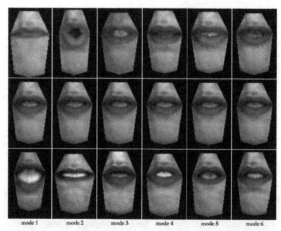

Fig. 6. Combined shape and appearance statistical model. The images show from left to right the first six most important components in PCA terminology. These modes account for 78.65% of the total variation. Centre row: Mean shape and appearance. Top row: Mean shape and appearance +2σ. Bottom row: Mean shape and appearance -2σ

4.2 Defining the feature vectors

The first approach towards lip reading and other similar problems was to use as visual features directly the AAM parameters. The other approach is to use the final results of the method, namely the co-ordinates of the landmarks as assigned by the algorithm for the current image. In our research we adopted this latter approach. Based on the position of the landmarks we defined seven high level geometric features. The features are computed as the Euclidean distances and areas between the certain key points that describe the shape of the mouth, namely mouth height and width, mouth aperture width and height, mouth area, aperture area and the nose to chin distance. The features are graphically described in Figure 7.

4.3 Visual validation of the feature vectors

Figure 8 shows the plots of the feature vectors computed for a random recording of the letter F having the viseme transcription [eeh fvw]. In this case the onset and offset moments of the utterance are clearly visible around the frame 75 and the frame 200 of the video recording, respectively. The onset of the viseme [eeh] is around the frame 80, while the onset of the viseme [fvw] is seen around frame 160. The actual shape of the mouth can be seen in the images shown below the graphs, which are extracted from the video sequence.

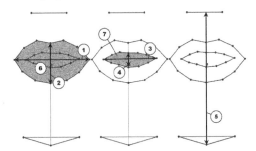

Fig. 7. The high level geometric features: 1) Outer lip width, 2) Outer lip height, 3) Inner lip width, 4) Inner lip height; 5) Chin to nose distance, 6) Outer lip area, 7) Inner lip area

Figure 9 shows the plots of the feature vectors for seven letters of the alphabet and the digit < 8 > ([a gkx td]). We see that the variability of the features is very high which makes them suitable for the recognition task at hand. We can also remark that, for instance, even though the viseme [aa] is present in the transcription of all letters, A([aa]), H([h aa]) and K([gkx aa]) we can clearly see that there is a slight difference between them with respect to the duration in each instance. This is best visible in the curve showing the height of the mouth, which shows that the duration of the viseme is shorter in the utterance of the letter K and H than in the case of the letter A.

An interesting result was obtained when visually inspecting the curves described by the feature vectors for all the visemes. By simple visual inspection we found that we could easily distinguish between some of the visemes, which proved that the feature set captures much of the speech related information. Table 6 summarises our findings in this respect. For a simple recognition task such as for instance the recognition of isolated visemes, or even the recognition of isolated digits, based on this table we could use a static classifier such as Support Vector Machines (SVM) (Ganapathiraju, 2002). However, for these types of classifiers the features need to be global features because they cannot handle time series. Therefore, the generalisation to longer and of variable length utterances is not possible.

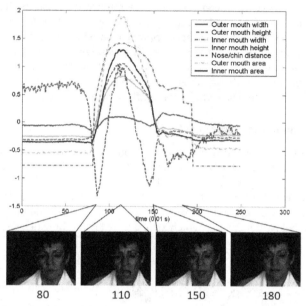

Fig. 8. The seven features plotted for one recording for the letter F transcribed using the visemes: eeh and fvw

	aa	h	gkx	a	oyu	ie	ei	iee	td	sz	eeh	l	pbm	fvw	at
Outer width	-		+	-	-	+	-+	+	+	+	+-	+-		+-	
Inner width	+		+	+		+	+	+			+		-		
Nose/chin dist	-	+	+	-	-	-	-	+-	+		+-	+-			
Height/area	+	+	+	+	-	+	+	+			+				

Table 6. Feature patterns per viseme: +) peak -) valley -+) increase +-) decrease.

4.4 AAM as ROI detection algorithm

It is worth mentioning that AAM can be used as well as a preprocess for defining a more accurate ROI. Therefore, the ROI defined using a mouth detection algorithm is further improved using the AAM. A more accurate ROI makes the data parametrization process more robust, because the background is better removed and, therefore, there is less noise in the input data.

5. Lip reading results

The method presented in this section produces for each frame in the corpus a vector with seven entries: mouth width, mouth height, aperture width, aperture height, mouth area, aperture area and the distance between the nose and the chin. We trained and tuned a lip reader based on the HMMs approach for each recognition task. In a similar approach, we considered both the case with simple static features (i.e. seven geometric features) and the case when the feature space was enriched with dynamic information consisting of deltas and accelerations (i.e. making 21-dimensional vectors). We trained systems based on mono-visemes as well as context aware tri-viseme systems. We used a Gaussian mixture arrangement to better describe the feature space and we performed a 10-fold validation in order to increase the confidence in the observed results. The best results obtained were WRR 90.32% with word accuracy 84.27% for the CD recognition task. In this case, 75% of the sequences was recognized correctly. Figure 10 shows the plot of the performance of the best recognizer as a function of the number of Gaussian mixtures used.

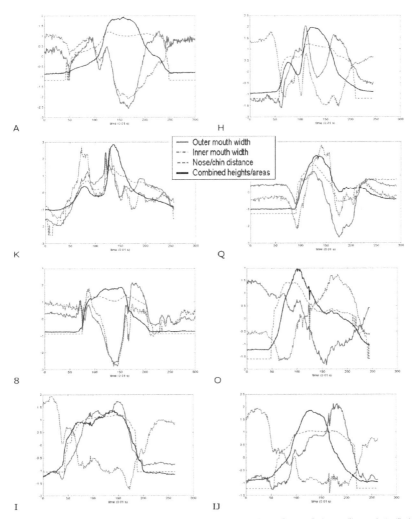

Fig. 9. Feature values plotted for the letters A ([aa]), H ([h aa]), K ([gkx aa]) and Q ([gkx oyu]), I ([ie]), O ([oyu]), IJ ([ei]) and 8 ([a gkx td]). The vectors are scaled using the time variance and centred around their mean

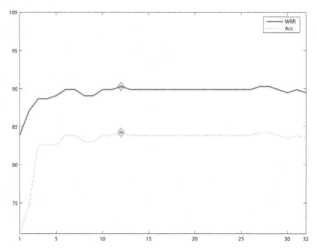

Fig. 10. The WRR and Acc results for CD recognition task as a function of the number of mixtures. The X axis gives the number of mixtures and the Y axis shows the results obtained. The feature vectors consisted of geometric features computed based on the AAM shape corroborated with their corresponding deltas and accelerations. The HMM models consisted of intra-word tri-visemes

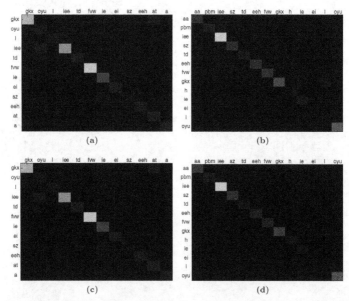

Fig. 11. The confusion matrices obtained by the best systems in the CD and CL tasks at the viseme level, respectively. a) the confusion matrix for CD task in the best case. b) the confusion matrix for CL task in the best case. c) the mean, over the mixture number, confusion matrix for the CD task. d) the mean, over the mixture number, confusion matrix for the CL task

For the GU recognition task we observed a 56% WRR. Using an N-Best approach with five most probable outcomes did not improve the result, which suggests the system is fairly robust. The 10-fold validation showed an 80.27% mean WRR with a 6% standard deviation, the minimum performance being 74.80% WRR. This shows some instability, however, the minimum is still a very good result. We also tested the results of the recognition at viseme level (i.e. before using the language model to build the corresponding words). This is useful for analysing the degree of confusion between different visemes. Figure 11 shows the confusion matrix for the best case. The mean confusion matrices computed over the mixture number is also displayed. We can remark in these figures that the degree of confusion is relatively small. However, the confusion is greater for visemes defined by larger phoneme sets. This is the case especially for the visemes [ɔyu] and [gkx] which are very often a source of confusion.

6. Conclusion

We introduced in this chapter an AAM based approach for lip reading. The AAM method is in our opinion a valuable tool for lip reading, both as a data parametrization method but also as a ROI detection technique. The method can be very robust and has a good generalization for unseen faces, however, the training process can be very long for satisfactory results to be obtained. Nevertheless, the shape obtained from the search scheme can be used as a starting point for testing other feature types, since it can always function as background elimination stencil. Based on the shape computed using the AAM searching scheme, we defined a set of high level geometric features. Based on these features we built different lip readers with very good results. These results validate the findings reported in the literature which showed that the width and the height of the mouth largely capture the content of the spoken utterance (Wojdel, 2003). This also justifies why a simple mouth model for lips synchronization based only on varying the mouth opening synchronous with the sound output is so convincing. We did not include in the feature vectors used in this chapter any information that describes the presence of the teeth, tongue or other elements of the mouth. This information was shown in the literature but also in our other experiments to be very important for lip reading. We expect that this is the case in the current settings as well. However, we did not include this information here because we wanted to have a clear understanding of the factors that influence the observed results.

7. References

Arsic, I. & Thiran, J.-P. (2006). *Mutual information eigenlips for audiovisual speech recognition*, In 14th European Signal Processing Conference (EU-SIPCO)

Atteveldt, N. van. (2006). *Speech meets script fMRI studies on the integration of letters and speech sounds*. Ph.D. thesis, Universiteit Maastricht

Beun, D. (1996). *Viseme syllable sets*, Master's thesis, Institute of Phonetic Sciences, University of Amsterdam

Boogaart, T.; Bos, L. & Bouer, L. (1994). *Use of the dutch polyphone corpus for application development*. In 2nd IEEE Workshop on Iterative Voice Technology for Telecomunication Applications. September

Breeuwer, M. (1985). *Speechreading Suplimented With Auditory Information*, Ph.D. thesis, Free University of Amsterdam

Bregler, C.; Hild, H. ; Manke, S. & Waibel, A. (1993). *Improving connected letter recognition by lipreading*. In IEEE International Conference on Acoustics Speech and Signal Processing, vol. 1. Institute of Electrical Engineers Inc (IEE)

Bregler, C. & Konig, Y. (1994). *Eigenlips for robust speech recognition*. In Acoustics, Speech, and Signal Processing, ICASSP-94 IEEE International Conference on

Buchan, J. N.; Pare, M. & Munhall, K. G. (2007). *Spatial statistics of gaze fixations during dynamic face processing*, Social Neuroscience, vol. 2(1), pp.1-13

Chibelushi, C. ; Gandon, S. ; Mason,J. ; Deravi, F. & Johnston, R. (1996). *Design issues for a digital audio-visual integrated database*, In Integrated Audio-Visual Processing for Recognition, Synthesis and Communication (Digest No: 1996/213), IEE Colloquium on

Chiou, G. I. & Hwang, J. N. (1997). *Lipreading from color video*, IEEE Transactions on Image Processing, vol. 6(8),pp. 1192-1195

Chitu, A. G. ; Rothkrantz, L.J.M. ; Wiggers, P. & Wojdel, J.C. (2007). *Comparison between different feature extraction techniques for audio-visual speech recognition*, In Journal on Multimodal User Interfaces, vol. 1,no. 1, pages 7-20, Springer, March

Chitu, A. G. & Rothkrantz, L. J. M. (2009). *The New Delft University of Technology Data Corpus for Audio-Visual Speech Recognition*. In Euromedia'2009, pp. 63-69. April

Chitu, A. G. ; Rothkrantz, L.J.M. (2009). *Visual Speech recognition- Automatic System for Lip Reading of Dutch*, In Journal on Information Technologies and Control, vol. year vii, no. 3, pages 2{9, Simolini-94, Sofia, Bulgaria

Cootes, T.; Edwards, G. & Taylor; C. (1998). *Active appearance models*, In H. Burkhardt and B. Neumann, editors, Proc. European Conference on Computer Vision 1998, vol. 2, pp. 484-498. Springer

Corthals , P. (1984). *Een eenvoudige visementaxonomie voor spraakafzien [a simple viseme taxonomy for lipreading]*, In Tijdscrijf Log en Audio, vol. 14, pp. 126-134

Daubias, P. & Deleglise, P. (2003). *The lium-avs database: a corpus to test lip segmentation and speechreading systems in natural conditions*, In Eighth European Conference on Speech Communication and Technology

Duchnowski, P.; Meier, U. & Waibel, A. (1994). *See me, hear me: Integrating automatic speech recognition and lip-reading.* Reading, vol. 1(1)

Duchnowski, P.; Hunke, M.; Büsching, D.; Meier, U. & Waibel, A. (1995). *Toward movement-invariant automatic lip-reading and speech recognition*, In International Conference on Acoustics, Speech, and Signal Processing, ICASSP-95, vol. 1, pp. 109-112

Dupont, S. & Luettin, J. (2000). *Audio-visual speech modeling for continuous speech recognition*, In IEEE Transactions On Multimedia, vol. 2. September

Eggermont, J. P. M. (1964). *Taalverwerving bij een Groep Dove Kinderen [Language Acquisition in a Group of Deaf Children]*

Eveno, N.; Caplier, A. & Coulon, P.-Y. (2004). *Automatic and accurate lip tracking*, In IEEE Transactions on Circuits and Systems for Video technology, vol. 15, pp. 706-715. May

Fisher, C. G. (1968). *Confusions among visually perceived consonants*, Journal of Speech, Language and Hearing Research, vol. 11(4), p. 796

Fleet, D. J.; Black, M. J.; Yacoob, Y. & Jepson, A. D. (2000). *Design and Use of Linear Models for Image Motion Analysis*, International Journal of Computer Vision, vol. 36(3), pp. 171-193

Furui, S. (2003). *Robust Methods in Automatic Speech Recognition and Understanding*, In EUROSPEECH 2003 - Geneva

Ganapathiraju, A. (2002). *Support vector machines for speech recognition*, Ph.D. thesis, Mississippi State University, Mississippi State, MS, USA, 2002. Major Professor-Picone, Joseph

Goecke, R.; Tran, Q. N.; Millar, J. B.; Zelinsky, A. & Robert-Ribes, J. (2000). *Validation of an automatic lip-tracking algorithm and design of a database for audio-video speech processing*, In Proc. 8th Australian Int. Conf. on Speech Science and Technology SST2000, pp. 92-97

Goecke, R.; Millar, J. B.; Zelinsky, A. & Robert-Ribes, J. (2000). *Automatic extraction of lip feature points*, In Proc. of the Australian Conference on Robotics and Automation ACRA2000, pp. 31-36

Goecke, R. & Millar, J. (2004). *The audio-video australian english speech data corpus avoze*, In Proceedings of the 8th International Conference on Spoken Language Processing ICSLP2004, vol. III, pp. 2525-2528. Jeju, Korea, October

Garofolo, J. (1988) *Getting started with the DARPA TIMIT CD-ROM: An acoustic phonetic continuous speech database*, National Institute of Standards and Technology (NIST), Gaithersburgh, MD, USA

Gray, M. S.; Movellan, J. R. & Sejnowski T. J. (1997). *Dynamic features for visual speechreading: A systematic comparison*, Advances in Neural Information Processing Systems, vol. 9, pp. 751-757

Hilder, S.; Harvey, R. & Theobald, B. J. (2009). *Comparison of human and machine-based lip-reading*, In B. J. Theobald and R. W. Harvey, editors, AVSP 2009, pp. 86-89. Norwich, September

Hong, X.; Yao, H.; Wan,Y. & Chen, R. (2006). *A PCA based visual DCT feature extraction method for lip-reading*, pp. 321-326

Iwano, K.; Tamura, S. & Furui, S. (2001). *Bimodal Speech Recognition Using Lip Movement Measured By Optical-Flow analysis*, In HSC2001

Kricke, R.; Gernoth, T. & Grigat, R.-R. (2008). *Local binary patterns for lip motion analysis.* In Image Processing 2008, 15th IEEE International Conference on, pp. 1472-1475

Kumar, K.; Chen, T. & Stern, R. M. (2007). *Profile view lip reading*, In Proceedings of the International Conference on Acoustics, Speech and Signal Processing ICASSP, vol. 4, pp. 429-432

Lee, B.; Hasegawa-Johnson, M.; Goudeseune, C.; Kamdar, S.; Borys, S.; Liu, M. & Huang, T. (2004). *Avicar: Audio-visual speech corpus in a car environment*, In INTERSPEECH2004-ICSLP. Jeju Island, Korea, October

Damhuis, M.; Boogaart, T.; Veld, C.; Versteijlen, M.; Schelvis, W.; Bos, L. & Boves, L. (1994). *Creation and analysis of the dutch polyphone corpus*, In Third International Conference on Spoken Language Processing. ISCA

Li, N.; Dettmer, S. & Shah, M. (1995). *Lipreading using eigen sequences*, In Proc. International Workshop on Automatic Face- and Gesture-Recognition, pp.30-34. Zurich, Switzerland

Li, N.; Dettmer, S. & Shah, M. (1997). *Visually recognizing speech using eigensequences*, Motion-based recognition, vol. 1, pp. 345-371

Lievin, M.; Delmas, P.; Coulon, P. Y.; Luthon, F. & Fristot, V. (1999). *Automatic lip tracking: Bayesian segmentation and active contours in a cooperative scheme*, In IEEE Conference on Multimedia, Computing and Systems, ICMCS99, vol. 1, pp. 691-696. Fiorenza, Italy, June

Lucey, P. & Potamianos, G. (2006). *Lipreading using profile versus frontal views*, In IEEE Multimedia Signal Processing Workshop, pp. 24-28

Luettin, J.; Thacker, N. A. & Beet, S. W. (1996). *Statistical lip modelling for visual speech recognition*, In Proceedings of the 8th European Signal Processing Conference (EUSIPCO96)

Luettin, J. & Thacker, N. A. (1997). *Speechreading using probabilistic models*, Computer Vision and Image Understanding, vol. 65(2), pp. 163-178

Martin, A. (1995). *Lipreading by optical flow correlation*, Technical report, Compute Science Department University of Central Florida

Mase, K. & Pentland, A. (1991). *Automatic lipreading by optical-flow analysis*, In Systems and Computers in Japan, vol. 22, pp. 67-76

Matthews, I. A.; Bangham, J. & Cox, S. J. (1996). *Audiovisual speech recognition using multiscale nonlinear image decomposition*, In Fourth International Conference on Spoken Language Processing

Matthews, I., Cootes, T. F.; Bangham, J. A.; Cox, S. & Harvey, R. (2002). *Extraction of visual features for lipreading*, In IEEE Transactions on Pattern Analysis and Machine Intelligence, vol. 24, pp. 198-213

Mcgurk, H. & Macdonald, J. (1976). *Hearing lips and seeing voices*, Nature, vol. 264, pp. 746-748, December

Messer, K.; Matas, J.; Kittler, J.; Luettin, J. & Maitre, G. (1999). *XM2VTSDB: The Extended M2VTS Database*, In Audio- and Video-based Biometric Person Authentication, AVBPA'99, pp. 72-77. Washington, D.C., March

Morn, L. E. L & Pinto-Elas, R. (2007). *Lips shape extraction via active shape model and local binary pattern*. MICAI 2007: Advances in Artificial Intelligence, vol. 4827, pp. 779-788

Movellan, J. R. (1995). *Visual Speech Recognition with Stochastic Networks*, In Advances in Neural Information Processing Systems, vol. 7. MIT Press, Cambridge

Nefian, A. V.; Liang, L.; Pi, X.; Liu, X. & Murphy, K. (2002). *Dynamic bayesian networks for audio-visual speech recognition*, EURASIP Journal on Applied Signal Processing, vol. 11, pp. 1274-1288

Neti, C.; Potamianos, G.; Luettin, J.; Matthews, I.; Glotin, H.; Vergyri, D.; Sison, J.; Mashari, A. & Zhou, J.(2000). *Audio-visual speech recognition*, In Final Workshop 2000 Report, vol. 764

Ojala, T. & Pietikainen, M. (1997). *Unsupervised texture segmentation using feature distributions*, Image Analysis and Processing, vol. 1310, pp. 311-318

Patterson, E.; Gurbuz, S. ; Tufekci, Z. & Gowdy, J. (2002). *CUAVE: A New Audio-Visual Database for Multimodal Human-Computer Interface Research*, In Proceedings of the IEEE International Conference on Acoustics, Speech, and Signal Processing

Petajan, E., Bischoff, B. & Bodoff, D. (1988). *An improved automatic lipreading system to enhance speech recognition*, In CHI '88: Proceedings of the SIGCHI conference on Human factors in computing systems, pp. 19-25. ACM Press, New York, NY, USA

Pigeon, S. & Vandendorpe, L. (1997). *The M2VTS multimodal face database(release 1.00)*, Lecture Notes in Computer Science, vol. 1206, pp. 403-410

Potamianos, G.; Cosatto, E.; Graf, H. & Roe, D. (1997). *Speaker independent audio-visual database for bimodal ASR*, In Proc. Europ. Tut. Work. Audio-Visual Speech Proc., Rhodes

Potamianos, G.; Graf, H. P. & Cosatto, E. (1998). *An image transform approach for hmm based automatic lipreading*, In Proc. IEEE International Conference on Image Processing, vol. 1

Potamianos, G.; Neti, C.; Luettin, J. & Matthews, I. (2004). *Audio-visual automatic speech recognition: An overview*, Issues in Visual and Audio-Visual Speech Processing

Prez, J. F. G.; Frangi, A. F.; Solano, E. L. & Lukas, K. (2005). *Lip reading for robust speech recognition on embedded devices*, In Int. Conf. Acoustics, Speech and Signal Processing, vol. I, pp. 473-476

Salazar, A.; Hernandez, J. & Prieto, F. (2007). *Automatic quantitative mouth shape analysis*, Lecture Notes in Computer Science, vol. 4673, pp. 416-421

Son van, N.; Huiskamp, T. M. I.; Bosman, A. J. & Smoorenburg, G. F. (1994). *Viseme classifications of Dutch consonants and vowels*, The Journal of the Acoustical Society of America, vol. 96

Tamura, S.; Iwano, K. & Furui, S. (2002). *A robust multi-modal speech recognition method using optical-flow analysis*, In Extended summary of IDS02, pp. 2-4. Kloster Irsee, Germany, June

Tamura, S.; Iwano, K. & Furui, S. (2004). *Multi-modal speech recognition using optical-flow analysis for lip images*, Journal VLSI Signal Process Systems, vol. 36(2-3), pp. 117-124

Tomlinson, M. J.; Russell, M. J. & Brooke, N. M. (1996). *Integrating audio and visual information to provide highly robust speech recognition*, In IEEE International Conference on Acoustics Speech and Signal Processing, vol. 2

Viola, P. & Jones, M. (2001). *Robust Real-time Object Detection*, In Second International Workshop On Statistical And Computational Theories Of Vision Modelling, Learning, Computing, And Sampling. Vancouver, Canada, July

Visser, M.; Poel, M. & Nijholt, A. (1999). *Classifying visemes for automatic Lipreading*, Lecture notes in computer science, pp. 349-352

Williams, J. J.; Rutledge, J. C. & Katsaggelos, A. K. (1998). *Frame rate and viseme analysis for multimedia applications to assist speechreading*. Journal of VLSI Signal Processing, vol. 20, pp. 7-23

Wojdel, J. C. & Rothkrantz, L. J. M. (2000). *Visually based speech onset/offset detection*, In Proceedings of 5th Annual Scientific Conference on Web Technology, New Media, Communications and Telematics Theory, Methods, Tools and Application (Euromedia 2000), pp. 156-160. Antwerp, Belgium

Wojdel, J.; Wiggers, P. & Rothkrantz, L.J.M. (2002). *An audio-visual corpus for multimodal speech recognition in dutch language*, In ICSLP, Conference Proceedings of

Wojdel, J. C. (2003). *Automatic Lipreading in the Dutch Language*, Ph.D. thesis, Delft University of Technology, November

Yoshinaga, T.; Tamura, S.; Iwano, K. & Furui, S. (2003). *Audio-Visual Speech Recognition Using Lip Movement Extracted from Side-Face Images*, In AVSP2003, pp. 117-120. September

Yoshinaga, T.; Tamura, S.; Iwano, K. & Furui, S. (2004). *Audio-visual speech recognition using new lip features extracted from side-face images*

Zhang, X.; Broun, C. C.; Mersereau, R. M. & Clements, M. A. (2002). *Automatic speechreading with applications to human-computer interfaces*, EURASIP Journal Appl Signal Process, vol. 2002(1), pp. 1228-1247

Zhao, G., Pietikäinen, M. & Hadid, A. (2007). *Local spatiotemporal descriptors for visual recognition of spoken phrases*, In Proceedings of the international workshop on Human-centered multimedia, pp. 66-75. ACM

7

Recognition of Emotion from Speech: A Review

S. Ramakrishnan

Department of Information Technology,
Dr. Mahalingam College of Engineering and Technology, Pollachi
India

1. Introduction

Emotional speech recognition is an area of great interest for human-computer interaction. The system must be able to recognize the user's emotion and perform the actions accordingly. It is essential to have a framework that includes various modules performing actions like speech to text conversion, feature extraction, feature selection and classification of those features to identify the emotions. The classifications of features involve the training of various emotional models to perform the classification appropriately. Another important aspect to be considered in emotional speech recognition is the database used for training the models. Then the features selected to be classified must be salient to identify the emotions correctly. The integration of all the above modules provides us with an application that can recognize the emotions of the user and give it as input to the system to respond appropriately.

In human interactions there are many ways in which information is exchanged (speech, body language, facial expressions, etc.). A speech message in which people express ideas or communicate has a lot of information that is interpreted implicitly. This information may be expressed or perceived in the intonation, volume and speed of the voice and in the emotional state of people, among others. The speaker's emotional state is closely related to this information. In evolutionary theory, it is widely accepted the "basic" term to define some emotions. The most popular set of basic emotions: happiness (joy), anger, fear, boredom, sadness, disgust and neutral. Over the last years the recognition of emotions has become a multi-disciplinary research area that has received great interest. This plays an important role in the improvement of human–machine interaction. Automatic recognition of speaker emotional state aims to achieve a more natural interaction between humans and machines. Also, it could be used to make the computer act according to the actual human emotion. This is useful in various real life applications as systems for real-life emotion detection using a corpus of agent-client spoken dialogues from a medical emergency call centre, detection of the emotional manifestation of fear in abnormal situations for a security application, support of semi-automatic diagnosis of psychiatric diseases and detection of emotional attitudes from child in spontaneous dialog interactions with computer characters. On the other hand, considering the other part of a communication system, progress was made in the context of speech synthesis too. The use of bio signals (such as ECG, EEG, etc.), face and body images are an interesting alternative to detect emotional states. However, methods to record and use these signals are more invasive, complex and impossible in certain real applications. Therefore, the use of speech signals clearly becomes a more feasible option. Good results are obtained by standard classifiers but their performance improvement could have reached a limit. Fusion, combination and ensemble of classifiers could represent a new step towards better emotion recognition systems.

This chapter aims to provide a comprehensive review on emotional speech recognition. The chapter is organized as follows. Section 2 describes the frameworks used for SER. Section 3 gives an overview of the types of databases. Section 4 presents the acoustic characteristics of emotions. Section 5 presents feature extraction and classification. Section 6 discusses the applications of emotion recognition. Section 7 presents concluding remarks.

2. Basic framework for emotional recognition

The input files are speech signals. Fig.1 gives the basic framework of emotional speech recognition. The feature extraction script extracts the features that represent global statistics. In the Post-processing step, the interface problem between the script for feature extraction and the feature selection technique can be solved. Then feature selection eliminates irrelevant features that hinder the recognition rates. It lowers the input dimensionality and saves the computational time. Distribution models like GMMs are trained using the most discriminative aspects of the feature. The classifiers distinguish the types of emotion.

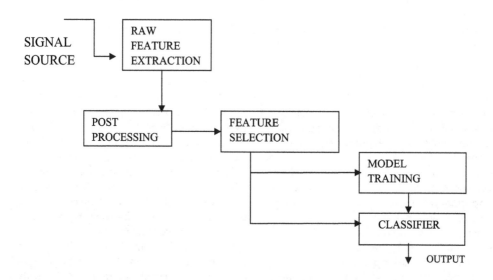

Fig. 1. Basic framework of SER

Bio signals such as ECG, EEG, GSR, face and body images are an interesting alternative to detect emotional states. Fig 2 discusses the mechanism of emotion recognition using these bio signals.

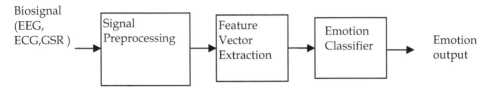

Fig. 2. Framework for emotion recognition using EEG,ECG,GSR signals

EEG is one of the most useful bio signals that detect true emotional state of human. The signal is recorded using the electrodes which measure the electrical activity of the brain. The recorded EEG data is first preprocessed to remove serious and obvious motion artifacts. Then the features are extracted from the raw signal using some feature extraction techniques like discrete wavelet transform, statistical based analysis etc. After the extraction the emotion classifier use the emotion classification techniques like Fuzzy C-Means, Quadratic Discriminant Analysis etc. to classify the different emotions of human.

ECG is recorded using ECG sensor .The signals are preprocessed using low pass filter at 100HZ. Then, features are extracted from the preprocessed signal by continuous wavelet transform (CWT) or discrete wavelets transform (DWT). Feature selection is done using Tabu Search Algorithm (TS), Simba algorithm etc. The selected feature is fed into classifier (fisher or K-Nearest Neighbor (KNN) classifier) to identify the type of emotion.

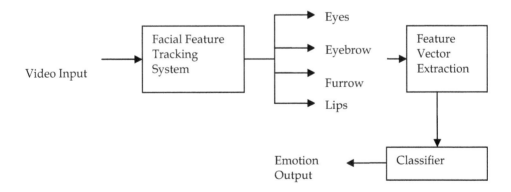

Fig. 3. Framework for Facial Emotional Recognition

Galvanic Skin Response is the measure of skin conductivity. There is a correlation between GSR and the arousal state of body. In the GSR emotional recognition system, the GSR signal is physiologically sensed and the feature is extracted using Immune Hybrid Particle Swarm Optimization (IH-PSO). The extracted features are classified using neural network classifier to identify the type of emotion.

In the facial emotion recognition the facial expression of a person is captured as a video and it is fed into the facial feature tracking system. Fig 3 gives a basic framework of facial emotional recognition.In facial feature tracking system, facial feature tracking algorithms such as Wavelets, Dual-view point-based model etc. are applied to track eyes, eyebrows, furrows and lips to collect all its possible movements. Then the extracted features are fed into classifier like Naïve Bayes , TAN or HMM to classify the type of emotion.

3. Emotional speech database

There should be some criteria that can be used to judge how well a certain emotional database simulates a real-world environment. According to some studies the following are the most relevant factors to be considered:

- Real-world emotions or acted ones
- Who utters the emotions
- How to simulate the utterances
- Balanced utterances or unbalanced utterances
- Utterances are uniformly distributed over emotions

Most of the developed emotional speech databases are not available for public use. Thus, there are very few benchmark databases that can be shared among researchers. Most of the databases share the following emotions: anger, joy, sadness, surprise, boredom, disgust, and neutral.

Types of DB

At the beginning of the research on automatic speech emotion recognition, acted speech was used and now it shifts towards more realistic data. The databases that are used in SER are classified into 3 types. Fig 4 briefs the types of databases. Table 1 gives a detailed list of speech databases.

Type 1 is acted emotional speech with human labeling. Simulated or acted speech is expressed in a professionally deliberated manner. They are obtained by asking an actor to speak with a predefined emotion, e.g. DES, EMO-DB.

Type 2 is authentic emotional speech with human labeling. Natural speech is simply spontaneous speech where all emotions are real. These databases come from real-life applications for example call-centers.

Type 3 is elicited emotional speech in which the emotions are induced with self-report instead of labeling, where emotions are provoked and self-report is used for labeling control. The elicited speech is neither neutral nor simulated.

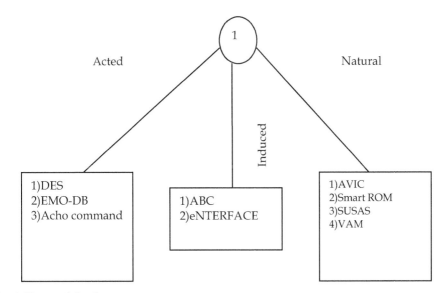

Fig. 4. Types of databases

S.No	Corpus Name	No.of Subjects (Total, Male, female and age and time & days taken)	Nature(Acted/Natural/ Induced and purpose, Language& mode)	Types of Emotions(Anger, disgust, fear, joy, sad, etc)	Publically Available(Yes/No) and URL
1	ABC (Airplane Behaviour Corpus)	Total=8 Age=25–48 years Time=8.4 s/431 clips	Nature=Acted purpose= Transport surveillance Language=German Mode=Audio-Visual	Aggressive, Cheerful,Intoxicated, Nervous, Neutral, Tired	Publically Available=No Detection of Security Related Affect and Behaviour in Passenger Transport
2	EMO(Berlin Emotional Database)	Total=10 Male = 5 Female = 5	Nature=Acted Purpose =General Language =German Mode=Audio	Anger, Boredom, Disgust, Fear, Joy, Neutral, Sadness	Publically Available=Yes http://pascal.kg w.tu-berlin.de/emodb /docu/#downlo ad
3	SUSAS(Speech Under Stimulated and Actual Stress)	Total=32 Male = 19 Female= 13 Age=22-76 years	Nature= Induced Language =English Purpose=Aircraft Mode=Audio	Fear ,High Stress, Medium Stress, Neutral	http://www.ldc. upenn.edu/Catal og/CatalogEntry .jsp?catalogId=L DC99S78
4	AVIC(Audiovis ual Interest Corpus)	Total=21 Male =11 Female = 10	Nature= Natural Language =English Mode=Audio-Visual		http://webcache .googleusercont ent.com/search?hl =en&start=10&q =cache:yp-tULzKJRwJ:http: //citeseerx.ist.ps

S.No	Corpus Name	No.of Subjects (Total, Male, female and age and time & days taken)	Nature(Acted/Natural/ Induced and purpose, Language& mode)	Types of Emotions(Anger, disgust, fear, joy, sad, etc)	Publicably Available(Yes/No) and URL
					u.edu/viewdoc/ download?doi=1 0.1.1.65.9121&rep =rep1&type=pdf +audiovisual+int erest+speech+dat abase&ct=clnk
5	SAL(Sensitive Artificial Listener)	Total=4 Female=2 Male=2 Time=20min/ speaker	Nature= Natural Purpose= Human-Computer conversation Language =English Mode=Audio-Visual		Publically Available=No http://emotion-research.net/toolb ox/toolboxdatabas e.2006-09-26.5667892524
6	Smartkom	Total =224 Time=4.5 min /person	Nature= Natural Purpose= Human-Computer conversation Language =German Mode=Audio-Visual	Neutral, Joy, Anger, Helplessness, Pondering, Surprise, Undefinable	Publically Available=No www.phonetik.u ni-muenchen.de/ Ba s/BasMultiModa leng.html#Smart Kom Linguistic nature of material=Interact ive discourse
7	VAM(Vera-Am-Mittag)	Total=47	Nature=Natural Language =German Mode=Audio-Visual	valence (negative vs. positive), activation (calm vs. excited) and dominance (weak vs. strong).	Publically Available=No http://emotion-research.net/down load/vam
8	DES(Danish Emotional Database)	Total=4 Male = 2 Female = 2 Age=18 -58 years old	Nature=Acted Purpose =General Language =Danish Mode=Audio	Anger, Happiness, Neutral, Sadness, Surprise	Publically Available=Yes http://universal. elra.info/product _info.php?produc ts_id=78
9	eNTERFACE	Total=42 Male = 34 Female = 8	Nature=Acted Purpose =General Language =English Mode=Audio-visual	Anger, Disgust, Fear, Joy, Sadness, Surprise	Publically Available=Yes Learning with synthesized speech for automatic emotion recognition
10	Groningen, 1996 ELRA corpus number S0020	Total=238	Nature=Acted Language = Dutch Mode=Audio		Publically Available=No www.elda.org/c atalogue/en/spe ech/S0020.html Linguistic nature of material= subjects read too

S.No	Corpus Name	No.of Subjects (Total, Male, female and age and time & days taken)	Nature(Acted/Natural/ Induced and purpose, Language& mode)	Types of Emotions(Anger, disgust, fear, joy, sad, etc)	Publicably Available(Yes/No) and URL
					short text with many quoted sentences to elicit emotional speech
11	Pereira (Pereira, 2000a,b)	Total =2	Nature=Acted Language = English Mode=Audio	Anger(hot), Anger(cold), Happiness, Neutrality, Sadness	Emotional Speech Recognition:Resources,Feature and Method Linguistic nature of material= 2 utterances(1 emotionally neutral sentence,4 digit number) each repeated
12	Van Bezooijen (Van Bezooijen, 1984)	Total =8 Male = 4 Female = 4	Nature=Acted Language = Dutch Mode=Audio	Anger, Contempt, Disgust, Fear, Interest, Joy, Neutrality, Sadness, Shame, Surprise	Linguistic nature of material=4 semantically neutral phrases
13	Alter (Alter et al.,2000)	Total =1	Nature=Acted Language = German Mode=Audio	Anger(cold), Happiness, Neutrality	Emotional Speech Recognition:Resources,Feature and Method Linguistic nature of material=3 sentences,1 for each emotion(with appropriate content)
14	Abelin (Abelin and Allwood,2000)	Total =1	Nature=Acted Language = Swedish Mode=Audio	Anger, Disgust, Dominance, Fear, Joy, Sadness, Shyness, Surprise	A State of Art Review on Emotional Speech Database Linguistic nature of material=1 semantically neutral phrase
15	Polzin (Polzin and Waibel,2000)	Unspecified number of speakers	Nature=Acted Language = English Mode=Audio-Visual	Anger, Sadness, Neutrality(other emotions as well,but in insuffient numbers to be used)	Emotional Speech Recognition:Resources,Feature and Method Linguistic nature of material=sentence length segments taken

S.No	Corpus Name	No.of Subjects (Total, Male, female and age and time & days taken)	Nature(Acted/Natural/ Induced and purpose, Language& mode)	Types of Emotions(Anger, disgust, fear, joy, sad, etc)	Publicably Available(Yes/No) and URL
					from acted movies
16	Banse and scherer (Banse and scherer,1996)	Total =12 Male = 6 Female = 6	Nature=Induced Language =German Mode=Audio-Visual	Anger(hot), Anger(cold), Anxiety, Boredom, Contempt, Disgust, Elation, Fear(panic), Happiness, Interest, Pride, Sadness, Shame	Linguistic nature of material=2 semantically neutral sentences(non-sense sentences composed of phonemes from Indo-European languages)
17	Mozziconacci (Mozziconacci 1998)	Total =3	Nature=Induced Language =Dutch Mode=Audio	Anger, Boredom, Fear, Disgust, Guilt, Happiness, Haughtiness, Indignation, Joy, Neutrality, Rage, Sadness, Worry	Linguistic nature of material=8 semantically neutral sentences(each repeated 3 times)
18	Iriondo et al. (Iriondo et al., 2000)	Total =8	Nature=Induced Language =Spanish Mode=Audio	Desire, Disgust, Fury, Fear, Joy, Surprise, Sadness	Emotional Speech Recognition:Resources,Feature and Method ,Linguistic nature of material=paragraph length passages(20-40mms each)
19	McGilloway (McGilloway,1997;Cowie and Douglas-Cowie,1996)	Total =40	Nature=Induced Language =English Mode=Audio	Anger, Fear, Happiness, Neutrality, Sadness	Linguistic nature of material= paragraph length passages
20	Belfast structured database	Total =50	Nature=Induced Language =English Mode=Audio	Anger, Fear, Happiness, Neutrality, Sadness	Linguistic nature of material= paragraph length passages written in first person
21	Amir et al. (Amir et al.,2000)	Total=61(60 Hebrew speakers and 1 Russian speaker)	Nature = Induced Language=Hebrew, Russian Mode=Audio	Anger, Disgust, Fear, Joy, Neutrality, Sadness	Linguistic nature of material=non-interactive discourse
22	Femandez et al.(Femandez and Picard,2000)	Total=4	Nature=Induced Language =English Mode=Audio	Stress	Linguistic nature of material=numerical answers to mathematical questions
23	Tolkmitt and Scherer	Total =60 Male = 33 Female	Nature=Induced Language =German	Stress(both cognitive and emotional)	Emotional Speech

S.No	Corpus Name	No.of Subjects (Total, Male, female and age and time & days taken)	Nature(Acted/Natural/ Induced and purpose, Language& mode)	Types of Emotions(Anger, disgust, fear, joy, sad, etc)	Publicably Available(Yes/No) and URL
	(Tolkmitt and Scherer,1986)	=27	Mode=Audio		Recognition:Resources,Feature and Method Linguistic nature of material=subjects made 3 vocal responses to each slide within a forty seconds presentation period-a numerical answer followed by 2 short statements. The start of each was scripted and subjects filled in the blank at the end.
24	Reading-Leeds database (Greasley et al.,1995;Roach et al.,1998)	Time=264 min	Nature=Natural Language =English Mode=Audio		Automated Extraction Of Annotation Data From The Reading/Leeds Emotional Speech Corpus Speech Research Laboratory,University of Reading, Reading, RG1 6AA, UK Linguistic nature of material=unscripted interactive discourse
25	Belfast natural database (Douglas-Cowie et al., 2000)	Total =125 Male = 31 Female =94	Nature=Natural Language =English Mode=Audio-Visual	Wide range	Publically available=no http://www.idiap.ch/mmm/corpora/emotion-corpus Linguistic nature of material= unscripted interactive discourse

S.No	Corpus Name	No.of Subjects (Total, Male, female and age and time & days taken)	Nature(Acted/Natural/ Induced and purpose, Language& mode)	Types of Emotions(Anger, disgust, fear, joy, sad, etc)	Publicably Available(Yes/No) and URL
26	Geneva Airport Lost Luggage Study (Scherer and Ceschi,1997, 2000)	Total =109	Nature=Natural Language =Mixed Mode=Audio-Visual	Anger, Good humour, Indifference, Stress, Sadness	http://www.uni ge.ch/fapse/emo tion/demo/Test Analyst/GERG/ apache/htdocs/i ndex.php Linguistic nature of material= unscripted interactive discourse
27	Chung (Chung,2000)	Total =77 (61 Korean speakers,6 American speakers)	Nature=Natural Language =Korean, English Mode=Audio-Visual	Joy, Neutrality, Sadness(distress)	Linguistic nature of material= interactive discourse
28	France et al.(France et al.,2000)	Total =115 Male = 67 Female =48	Nature=Natural Language =English Mode=Audio	Depression, Neutrality, Suicidal state	Publically Available=no http://emotion-research.net/Mem bers/admin/test/ ?searchterm=Franc e%20et%20al.(Fran ce%20et%20al.,200 0) Linguistic nature of material= interactive discourse
29	Slaney and McRoberts (1998) or Breazeal (2001)	Total =6	Nature=Acted Language =English, Japanese Purpose=pet robot Mode=Audio	Joy, Sadness, Anger, Neutrality	Publically Available=no
30	FAU Aibo Database	Total=26 children Male=13 Female=13	Nature=Natural Language =German Purpose=pet robot	Anger, Emphatic, Neutral, Positive, and Rest	Publically Available=no http://www5.cs. fau.de/de/mitar beiter/steidl-stefan/fau-aibo-emotion-corpus/
31	SALAS database	Total=20	Nature=Induced Language =English Mode=Audio-Visual	Wide range	Publically Available=no http://www.ima ge.ntua.gr/ermis / IST-2000-29319, D09 Linguistic nature of material= interactive discourse

Table 1. List of emotional speech databases

4. Acoustic characteristics of emotions in speech

The prosodic features like pitch, intensity, speaking rate and voice quality are important to identify the different types of emotions. In particular pitch and intensity seem to be correlated to the amount of energy required to express a certain emotion. When one is in a state of anger, fear or joy; the resulting speech is correspondingly loud, fast and enunciated with strong high-frequency energy, a higher average pitch, and wider pitch range, whereas with sadness, producing speech that is slow, low-pitched, and with little high-frequency energy. In Table 2, a short overview of acoustic characteristics of various emotional states is provided.

EMOTIONS / CHARACTERISTICS	JOY	ANGER	SADNESS	FEAR	DISGUST
Pitch mean	High	very high	very low	very high	very low
Pitch range	High	high	Low	High	high-male low-female
Pitch variance	High	very high	Low	very high	Low
Pitch contour	incline	decline	Decline	Incline	Decline
Intensity mean	High	very high-male high-female	Low	medium/ high	Low
Intensity range	High	high	Low	High	Low
Speaking Rate	High	low-male high-female	high-male low-female	High	very low-male low-female
Transmission Durability	Low	low	High	Low	High
Voice Quality	modal/ tense	Sometimes breathy; Moderately blaring timbre	Resonant timbre	Falsetto	Resonant timbre

Table 2. Acoustic Characteristics of Emotions

5. Feature extraction and classification

The collected emotional data usually contain noise due to the background and "hiss" of the recording machine. The presence of noise will corrupt the signal, and make the feature extraction and classification less accurate. Thus preprocessing of speech signal is very much required. Preprocessing also reduces the variability.

Normalization is a preprocessing technique that eliminates speaker and recording variability while keeping the emotional discrimination. Generally 2 types of normalization techniques are performed they are energy normalization and pitch normalization. Energy normalization: the speech files are scaled such that the average RMS energy of the neutral reference database and the neutral subset in the emotional databases are the same for each speaker. This normalization is separately applied for each subject in each database. The goal of this normalization is to compensate for different recording settings among the databases. Pitch normalization: the pitch contour is normalized for each subject (speaker-dependent normalization). The average pitch across speakers in the neutral reference database is estimated. Then, the average pitch value for the neutral set of the emotional databases is estimated for each speaker.

Feature extraction involves simplifying the amount of resources required to describe a large set of data accurately. When performing analysis of complex data one of the major problems stems from the number of variables involved. Analysis with a large number of variables generally requires a large amount of memory and computation power or a classification algorithm which overfits the training sample and generalizes poorly to new samples. Feature extraction is a general term for methods of constructing combinations of the variables to get around these problems while still the data with sufficient accuracy.

Although significant advances have been made in speech recognition technology, it is still a difficult problem to design a speech recognition system for speaker-independent, continuous speech. One of the fundamental questions is whether all of the information necessary to distinguish words is preserved during the feature extraction stage. If vital information is lost during this stage, the performance of the following classification stage is inherently crippled and can never measure up to human capability. Typically, in speech recognition, we divide speech signals into frames and extract features from each frame. During feature extraction, speech signals are changed into a sequence of feature vectors. Then these vectors are transferred to the classification stage. For example, for the case of dynamic time warping (DTW), this sequence of feature vectors is compared with the reference data set. For the case of hidden Markov models (HMM), vector quantization may be applied to the feature vectors which can be viewed as a further step of feature extraction. In either case, information loss during the transition from speech signals to a sequence of feature vectors must be kept to a minimum. There have been numerous efforts to develop good features for speech recognition in various circumstances.

The most common speech characteristics that are extracted are categorized in the following groups:

Frequency characteristics

- Accent shape – affected by the rate of change of the fundamental frequency.
- Average pitch – description of how high/low the speaker speaks relative to the normal speech.
- Contour slope – describes the tendency of the frequency change over time, it can be rising, falling or level.
- Final lowering – the amount by which the frequency falls at the end of an utterance.
- Pitch range – measures the spread between maximum and minimum frequency of an utterance.
- Formant-frequency components of human speech
- MFCC-representation of the short-term power spectrum of a sound, based on a linear cosine transform of a log power spectrum on a nonlinear mel scale of frequency.
- Spectral features- measures the slope of the spectrum considered.

Time-related features

- Speech rate – describes the rate of words or syllables uttered over a unit of time
- Stress frequency – measures the rate of occurrences of pitch accented utterances
- Energy- Instantaneous values of energy
- Voice quality- jitter and shimmer of the glottal pulses of the whole segment.

Voice quality parameters and energy descriptors

- Breathiness – measures the aspiration noise in speech
- Brilliance – describes the dominance of high Or low frequencies In the speech
- Loudness – measures the amplitude of the speech waveform, translates to the energy of an utterance
- Pause Discontinuity – describes the transitions between sound and silence
- Pitch Discontinuity – describes the transitions of fundamental frequency.

Durational pause related features :The duration features include the chunk length, measured in seconds, and the zero-crossing rate to roughly decode speaking rate. Pause is obtained as the proportion of non-speech to the speech signal calculated by a voice activity detection algorithm

Zipf features used for a better rhythm and prosody characterization.

Hybrid pitch features combines outputs of two different speech signal based pitch marking algorithms (PMA)

Feature selection determines which features are the most beneficial because most classifiers are negatively influenced by redundant, correlated or irrelevant features. Thus, in order to reduce the dimensionality of the input data, a feature selection algorithm is implemented to choose the most significant features of the training data for the given task. Alternatively, a feature reduction algorithm like principal components analysis (PCA) and Sequential Forward Floating Search (SFFS) can be used to encode the main information of the feature space more compactly.

Most research on SER has concentrated on feature-based and classification-based approaches. Feature-based approaches aim at analyzing speech signals and effectively estimating feature parameters representing human emotional states. The classification-based approaches focus on designing a classifier to determine distinctive boundaries between emotions. The process of emotional speech detection also requires the selection of a successful classifier which will allow for quick and accurate emotion identification. Currently, the most frequently used classifiers are linear discriminant classifiers (LDC), k-nearest neighbor (k-NN), Gaussian mixture model (GMM), support vector machines (SVM), decision tree algorithms and hidden Markov models (HMMs).Various studies showed that choosing the appropriate classifier can significantly enhance the overall performance of the system.

The list below gives a brief description of each algorithm:

LDC: A linear classifier uses the feature values to identify which class (or group) it belongs to by making a classification decision based on the value of a linear combination of the feature values .They are usually presented to the system in a vector called a feature vector.

k-NN: Classification happens by locating the instance in feature space and comparing it with the k nearest neighbors (training examples) and labeling the unknown feature with the same class label as that of the located (known) neighbor. The majority vote decides the outcome of class labeling.

GMM: A model of the probability distribution of the features measured in a biometric system such as vocal-tract related spectral features in a speaker recognition system. It is used for representing the existence of sub-populations, which is described using the mixture distribution, within the overall population.

SVM : It is a binary classifier to analyze the data and recognize the patterns for classification and regression analysis.

Decision tree algorithms: work based on following a decision tree in which leaves represent the classification outcome, and branches represent the conjunction of subsequent features that lead to the classification.

HMMs: It is a generalized model in which the hidden variables control the components to be selected. The hidden variables are related through the Markov process. In the case of emotion recognition, the outputs represent the sequence of speech feature vectors, which allow the deduction of states' sequences through which the model progressed. The states can consist of various intermediate steps in the expression of an emotion, and each of them has a probability distribution over the possible output vectors. The states' sequences allow us to predict the emotional state which we are trying to classify, and this is one of the most commonly used techniques within the area of speech affect detection.

Boostexter: an iterative algorithm that is based on the principle of combining many simple and moderately inaccurate rules into a single, highly accurate rule. It focuses on text categorization tasks. An advantage of Boostexter is that it can deal with both continuous-valued input (e.g., age) and textual input (e.g., a text string).

6. Applications

Emotion detection is a key phase in our ability to use users' speech and communications as a source of important information on users' needs, desires, preferences and intentions. By recognizing the emotional content of users' communications, marketers can customize offerings to users even more precisely than ever before .This is an exciting innovation that is destined to add an interesting dimension to the man-machine interface, with unlimited potential for marketing as well as consumer products, transportation, medical and therapeutic applications, traffic control and so on.

Intelligent Tutoring System: It aims to provide intervention strategies in response to a detected emotional state, with the goal being to keep the student in a positive affect realm to maximize learning potential. The research follows an ethnographic approach in the determination of affective states that naturally occur between students and computers. The multimodal inference component will be evaluated from audio recordings taken during classroom sessions. Further experiments will be conducted to evaluate the affect component and educational impact of the intelligent tutor.

Lie Detection: Lie Detector helps in deciding whether someone is lying or not. This mechanism is used particularly in areas such as Central Bureau of Investigation for finding out the criminals, cricket council to fight against corruption. **X13-VSA PRO Voice Lie Detector 3.0.1 PRO** is an innovative, advanced and sophisticated software system and a fully computerized voice stress analyzer that allows us to detect the truth instantly.

Banking: The ATM will employ speaker recognition and authentication if needed "to ensure higher security level while accessing to confidential data." In other words, the unique deployment of combining speech recognition, speaker recognition and emotion detection is not designed to be spooky or invasive. "It is just one more step forward the creation of humanlike systems that speak to the clients, understand and recognize a speaker". What's different is the incorporation of emotion detection in the enrollment process, which is probably a very good idea if enrollments are going to be conducted without human assistance or supervision. The machine will be able to talk with the prospective enrollee (and later on the client) and will be able to authenticate his or her unique voiceprint while, at the same time, test voice levels for signs of nervousness, anger, or deceit.

In-Car Board System: An in-car board system shall be provided with information about the emotional state of the driver to initiate safety strategies, initiatively provide aid or resolve errors in the communication according to the driver's emotion.

Prosody in Dialog System: We investigate the use of prosody for the detection of frustration and annoyance in natural human-computer dialog. In addition to prosodic features, we examine the contribution of language model information and speaking "style". Results show that a prosodic model can predict whether an utterance is neutral versus "annoyed or frustrated" with an accuracy on par with that of human interlobular agreement. Accuracy increases when discriminating only "frustrated" from other utterances, and when using only those utterances on which labelers originally agreed. Furthermore, prosodic model accuracy degrades only slightly when using recognized versus true words. Language model features, even if based on true words, are relatively poor predictors of frustration.

Emotion Recognition in Call Center: Call-centers often have a difficult task of managing customer disputes. Ineffective resolution of these disputes can often lead to customer discontent, loss of business and in extreme cases, general customer unrest where a large amount of customers move to a competitor. It is therefore important for call-centers to take note of isolated disputes and effectively train service representatives to handle disputes in a way that keeps the customer satisfied.

A system was designed to monitor recorded customer messages and provide an emotional assessment for more effective call-back prioritization. However, this system only provided post-call classification and was not designed for real time support or monitoring. Nowadays the systems are different because it aims to provide a real-time assessment to aid in the handling of the customer while he or she is speaking. Early warning signs of customer frustration can be detected from pitch contour irregularities, short-time energy changes, and changes in the rate of speech.

Sorting of Voice Mail: Voicemail is an electronic system for recording and storing of voice messages for later retrieval by the intended recipient. It would be a potential application to sort the voice mail according to the emotion of the person's voice recorded. It will help to respond to the caller appropriately.

Computer Games: Computer games can be controlled through emotions of human speech. The computer recognizes human emotion from their speech and compute the level of game (easy, medium, hard). For example, if the human speech is in form of aggressive nature then the level becomes hard. Suppose if the human is too relaxed the level becomes easy. The rest of emotions come under medium level.

Diagnostic Tool By Speech Therapists: Person who diagnosis and treats variety of speech, voice, and language disorders is called a Speech Therapist. By understanding and empathizing emotional stress and strains the therapists can know what the patient is suffering from. The software used for recording and analyzing the entire speech is icSpeech. The use of speech communication in healthcare is to allow the patient to describe their health condition to the best of their knowledge. In clinical analysis, human emotions are analyzed based on features related to prosodics, the vocal tract, and parameters extracted directly from the glottal waveform. Emotional expressions can be referred by vocal affect extracted from the human speech.

Robots: Robots can interact with people and assist them in their daily routines, in common places such as homes, super markets, hospitals or offices. For accomplishing these tasks, robots should recognize the emotions of the humans to provide a friendly environment. Without recognizing the emotion, the robot cannot interact with the human in a natural way.

7. Conclusion

The process of speech emotion detection requires the creation of a reliable database, broad enough to fit every need for its application, as well as the selection of a successful classifier which will allow for quick and accurate emotion identification. Thirty-one emotional speech databases are reviewed. Each database consists of a corpus of human speech pronounced under different emotional conditions. A basic description of each database and its applications is provided. And the most common emotions searched for in decreasing frequency of appearance are anger, sadness, happiness, fear, disgust, joy, surprise, and boredom. The complexity of the emotion recognition process increases with the amount of emotions and features used within the classifier. It is therefore crucial to select only the most relevant features in order to assure the ability of the model to successfully identify emotions, as well as increasing the performance, which is particularly significant to real-time detection. SER has in the last decade shifted from a side issue to a major topic in human computer interaction and speech processing. SER has potentially wide applications. For example, human computer interfaces could be made to respond differently according to the emotional state of the user. This could be especially important in situations where speech is the primary mode of interaction with the machine.

8. References

[1] Zhihong Zeng, Maja Pantic I. Roisman, and Thomas S. Huang, 'A Survey of Affect Recognition Methods: Audio,Visual, and Spontaneous Expressions', IEEE

Transactions on Pattern Analysis and Machine Intelligence, Vol. 31, No. 1, pp.39-58, January 2009.

[2] Panagiotis C. Petrantonakis , and Leontios J. Hadjileontiadis, ' Emotion Recognition From EEG Using Higher Order Crossings', IEEE Trans. on Information Technology In Biomedicine, Vol. 14, No. 2,pp.186-197, March 2010.

[3] Christos A. Frantzidis, Charalampos Bratsas, et al 'On the Classification of Emotional Biosignals Evoked While Viewing Affective Pictures: An Integrated Data-Mining-Based Approach for Healthcare Applications', IEEE Trans. on Information Technology In Biomedicine, Vol. 14, No. 2, pp.309-318,March 2010

[4] Yuan-Pin Lin, Chi-Hong Wang, Tzyy-Ping Jung, Tien-Lin Wu, Shyh-Kang Jeng, Jeng-Ren Duann, , and Jyh-Horng Chen, 'EEG-Based Emotion Recognition in Music Listening', IEEE Trans. on Biomedical Engineering, Vol. 57, No. 7, pp.1798-1806 , July 2010.

[5] Meng-Ju Han, Jing-Huai Hsu and Kai-Tai Song, A New Information Fusion Method for Bimodal Robotic Emotion Recognition, Journal of Computers, Vol. 3, No. 7, pp.39-47, July 2008

[6] Claude C. Chibelushi, Farzin Deravi, John S. D. Mason, 'A Review of Speech-Based Bimodal Recognition', IEEE Transactions On Multimedia, vol. 4, No. 1 ,pp.23-37,March 2002.

[7] Bjorn Schuller , Bogdan Vlasenko, Florian Eyben , Gerhard Rigoll , Andreas Wendemuth, 'Acoustic Emotion Recognition:A Benchmark Comparison of Performances', IEEE workshop on Automatic Speech Recognition and Understanding , pp.552-557, Merano,Italy, December 13-20,2009.

[8] Ellen Douglas-Cowie , Nick Campbell , Roddy Cowie , Peter Roach, 'Emotional Speech: Towards a New Generation Of Databases' , Speech Communication Vol. 40, pp.33-60 ,2003.

[9] John H.L. Hansen, 'Analysis and Compensation of Speech under Stress and Noise for Environmental Robustness in Speech Recognition', Speech Communication, Special Issue on Speech Under Stress,vol. 20(1-2), pp. 151-170, November 1996.

[10] Carlos Busso, , Sungbok Lee, , and Shrikanth Narayanan, , 'Analysis of Emotionally Salient Aspects of Fundamental Frequency for Emotion Detection', IEEE Transactions on Audio, Speech, and Language Processing, Vol. 17, No. 4, pp.582-596, May 2009.

[11] Nathalie Camelin, Frederic Bechet, Géraldine Damnati, and Renato De Mori, ' Detection and Interpretation of Opinion Expressions in Spoken Surveys', IEEE Transactions On Audio, Speech, And Language Processing, Vol. 18, No. 2, pp.369-381, February 2010.

[12] Dimitrios Ververidis , Constantine Kotropoulos, 'Fast and accurate sequential floating forward feature selection with the Bayes classifier applied to speech emotion recognition',Elsevier Signal Processing, vol.88,issue 12,pp.2956-2970,2008

[13] K B khanchandani and Moiz A Hussain, 'Emotion Recognition Using Multilayer Perceptron And Generalized Feed Forward Neural Network', IEEE Journal Of Scientific And Industrial Research Vol.68, pp.367-371,May 2009

[14] Tal Sobol-Shikler, and Peter Robinson, 'Classification of Complex Information: Inference of Co-Occurring Affective States from Their Expressions in Speech', IEEE

Transactions On Pattern Analysis And Machine Intelligence, Vol. 32, No. 7, pp.1284-1297, July 2010

[15] Daniel Erro, Eva Navas, Inma Hernáez, and Ibon Saratxaga, 'Emotion Conversion Based on Prosodic Unit Selection' , IEEE Transactions On Audio, Speech And Language Processing, Vol. 18, No. 5, pp.974-983, July 2010

[16] Khiet P. Truong and Stephan Raaijmakers, 'Automatic Recognition of Spontaneous Emotions in Speech Using Acoustic and Lexical Features', MLMI 2008, LNCS 5237, pp. 161–172, 2008.

[17] Bjorn Schuller, Gerhard Rigoll, and Manfred Lang, 'Speech Emotion Recognition Combining Acoustic Features and Linguistic Information in a Hybrid Support Vector Machine - Belief Network Architecture', IEEE International Conference on Acoustics, Speech, and Signal Processing, Quebec,Canada,17-21 May,2004

[18] Bjorn Schuller, Bogdan Vlasenko, Dejan Arsic, Gerhard Rigoll, Andreas Wendemuth, 'Combining Speech Recognition and Acoustic Word Emotion Models for Robust text-Independent Emotion Recognition', IEEE International Conference on Multimedia & Expo,Hannover,Germany,June 23-26,2008

[19] Wernhuar Tarng, Yuan-Yuan Chen, Chien-Lung Li, Kun-Rong Hsie and Mingteh Chen, 'Applications of Support Vector Machines on Smart Phone Systems for Emotional Speech Recognition', World Academy of Science, Engineering and Technology Vol.72, pp.106-113, 2010

[20] Silke Paulmann , Marc D. Pell , Sonja A. Kotz, 'How aging affects the recognition of emotional speech', Brain and Language Vol. 104, pp.262–269,2008

[21] Elliot Moore II, Mark A. Clements, , John W. Peifer, , and Lydia Weisser , 'Critical Analysis of the Impact of Glottal Features in the Classification of Clinical Depression in Speech', IEEE Transactions On Biomedical Engineering,Vol. 55, No. 1, pp.96-107, January 2008.

[22] Yongjin Wang and Ling Guan, Recognizing Human Emotional State From Audiovisual Signals, IEEE Transactions on Multimedia, Vol. 10, No. 4, pp. 659-668, June 2008.

Permissions

The contributors of this book come from diverse backgrounds, making this book a truly international effort. This book will bring forth new frontiers with its revolutionizing research information and detailed analysis of the nascent developments around the world.

We would like to thank S. Ramakrishnan, for lending his expertise to make the book truly unique. He has played a crucial role in the development of this book. Without his invaluable contribution this book wouldn't have been possible. He has made vital efforts to compile up to date information on the varied aspects of this subject to make this book a valuable addition to the collection of many professionals and students.

This book was conceptualized with the vision of imparting up-to-date information and advanced data in this field. To ensure the same, a matchless editorial board was set up. Every individual on the board went through rigorous rounds of assessment to prove their worth. After which they invested a large part of their time researching and compiling the most relevant data for our readers. Conferences and sessions were held from time to time between the editorial board and the contributing authors to present the data in the most comprehensible form. The editorial team has worked tirelessly to provide valuable and valid information to help people across the globe.

Every chapter published in this book has been scrutinized by our experts. Their significance has been extensively debated. The topics covered herein carry significant findings which will fuel the growth of the discipline. They may even be implemented as practical applications or may be referred to as a beginning point for another development. Chapters in this book were first published by InTech; hereby published with permission under the Creative Commons Attribution License or equivalent.

The editorial board has been involved in producing this book since its inception. They have spent rigorous hours researching and exploring the diverse topics which have resulted in the successful publishing of this book. They have passed on their knowledge of decades through this book. To expedite this challenging task, the publisher supported the team at every step. A small team of assistant editors was also appointed to further simplify the editing procedure and attain best results for the readers.

Our editorial team has been hand-picked from every corner of the world. Their multi-ethnicity adds dynamic inputs to the discussions which result in innovative outcomes. These outcomes are then further discussed with the researchers and contributors who give their valuable feedback and opinion regarding the same. The feedback is then collaborated with the researches and they are edited in a comprehensive manner to aid the understanding of the subject.

Apart from the editorial board, the designing team has also invested a significant amount of their time in understanding the subject and creating the most relevant covers. They scrutinized every image to scout for the most suitable representation of the subject and create an appropriate cover for the book.

The publishing team has been involved in this book since its early stages. They were actively engaged in every process, be it collecting the data, connecting with the contributors or procuring relevant information. The team has been an ardent support to the editorial, designing and production team. Their endless efforts to recruit the best for this project, has resulted in the accomplishment of this book. They are a veteran in the field of academics and their pool of knowledge is as vast as their experience in printing. Their expertise and guidance has proved useful at every step. Their uncompromising quality standards have made this book an exceptional effort. Their encouragement from time to time has been an inspiration for everyone.

The publisher and the editorial board hope that this book will prove to be a valuable piece of knowledge for researchers, students, practitioners and scholars across the globe.

List of Contributors

Rudy Rotili, Emanuele Principi, Stefano Squartini and Francesco Piazza
Università Politecnica delle Marche, Italy

Trabelsi Abdelaziz, Boyer François-Raymond and Savaria Yvon
École Polytechnique de Montréal, Canada

Nefissa Annabi-Elkadri, Atef Hamouda and Khaled Bsaies
URPAH Research Unit, Computer Science Department, Faculty of Sciences of Tunis, Tunis El Manar University, Tunis, Tunisia

N. R. Raajan and T. R. Sivaramakrishnan
School of Electrical and Elcetronics Engineering, SASTRA University, Thanjore, India

Y. Venkatramani
Saranathan College of Engineering, Trichy, India

Jani Nurminen
Accenture, Finland

Hanna Silén, Victor Popa, Elina Helander and Moncef Gabbouj
Tampere University of Technology, Finland

Alin Chiţu and Léon J.M. Rothkrantz
Delft University of Technology, The Netherlands

Léon J.M. Rothkrantz
Netherlands Defence Academy, The Netherlands

S. Ramakrishnan
Department of Information Technology, Dr. Mahalingam College of Engineering and Technology, Pollachi, India

Printed in the USA
CPSIA information can be obtained
at www.ICGtesting.com
JSHW011332221024
72173JS00003B/132

9 781632 404718